8/08

CAMP CAMP

CAMP CAMP

Where Fantasy Island Meets
Lord of the Flies

Roger Bennett and Jules Shell

Crown Publishers/New York

Henry Jacobs
Utica, MS
c. 1984

Published in the United States by Crown Publishers, an imprint of the
Crown Publishing Group, a division of Random House, Inc., New York.
www.crownpublishing.com

Crown is a trademark and the Crown colophon is a registered trademark of
Random House, Inc.

Library of Congress Cataloging-in-Publication Data is available upon request.

ISBN 978-0-307-38262-7

Printed in China

Design by Nove Studio
Cover photo courtesy of Kevin Harrison
Back cover photos courtesy of Perry Silver (top),
Gillian Laub (middle), and Liz Stevens (bottom)

The names and identifying characteristics of some of the people mentioned in
this book have been changed in an effort to minimize intrusions on their privacy.

10 9 8 7 6 5 4 3 2 1

First Edition

To camp directors across the country—
especially those of Camp Walden, Denmark, Maine,
for ensuring that every day with Vanessa felt like the
best one of the summer at camp

In loving memory of Jon "Goobie" Goldberg,
legendary counselor, 1967–2007, page 145

CONTENTS

Foreword

BY IVAN REITMAN

Between the ages of seven and fifteen, going to summer camp was the most important influence in my life. The opportunity to be away from my parents and live with a gang of kids in the country was the perfect way to spend a summer.

I honestly believe that I would not have the life or career that I now have had I not gone to camp. It was at camp that I started my first band, acted in a play, competed in group sports, and learned that one can actually talk to members of the opposite sex.

The movie *Meatballs* came about virtually by accident. The idea for the film came to me shortly after the first screening of *National Lampoon's Animal House.* It was clear from this screening that the film was destined to be a success. I called up my old friends Dan Goldberg and Len Blum and suggested that we create a movie about summer camp based on our personal experiences.

Remarkably, just three months after that phone call, I was deep into pre-production for my summer camp movie, soon to be known as *Meatballs.* We convinced the owner of Camp White Pine in Haliburton, Ontario, to let us shoot there while camp was in session. This is what gives the movie its authenticity. I shot real kids doing real camp stuff while the extraordinary (and then unknown) Bill Murray played counterpoint.

When I look back on *Meatballs* now, more than twenty-five years later, I am pleased with how honestly and joyfully it reflected my own camp experiences: from crying as a seven-year-old when my parents left me after Visiting Day to the shivering excitement I experienced after my first kiss to the thrill of competing in Color War. All of the feelings I felt during and about summer camp are woven into that movie.

Looking at the terrific photographs in this book brings back these beautiful memories, and I hope that you and your children will experience this pleasure as well.

Introduction

This book is about summer camp in the same way Plato's *Cave* is about prisoners in chains, or "Hungry Like the Wolf" is about the animal kingdom. On the surface, this is the tale of the great American institution of sleepaway camp, a parallel universe filled with bunk mates, unrequited crushes, appropriated Native American terminology, competitive sports, libido-soaked socials, panty raids, and snugly fitted velour shorts topped off with tube socks. But underneath, it is nothing less than the story of our generation and how we got to be this way, picking up where our first book, *Bar Mitzvah Disco,* left off. If that book was about one night of adolescent madness played out against a backdrop of family and friends, summer camp is the logical next chapter—the one or two golden months a year in which young Americans escaped the smothering embrace of home to travel far away from everything that was familiar. Summer camp was the chance to leave the grind of the city or crushing boredom of the suburbs to embrace the green fields and freshwater lakes of camp, where they could create temporary teenage utopias, run by kids, for kids.

We have spent the past two years piecing this story together via photographs, tall tales, and tie-dye T-shirts that were sent to us from around the country. As we near the end of the process, we are happy to be able to confirm that summer camp is the definitive formative experience for our generation, performing a role similar to the one Woodstock, Pearl Harbor, and the Boston Tea Party played for our parents and grandparents. This claim is based on our scientific research, in which we uncovered vast networks of former campers scattered across North America, each more eager than the last to catalog the ways in which camp has made them who they are today. Their number, fanaticism, and collective power are staggering, equaling that of Opus Dei, the Masons, and Simon Cowell combined. While most have gone on to create what could pass for normal lives on the surface, many admitted they were still ready to respond to a Color War breakout at a moment's notice.

Jules Shell
Camp Walden
Cheboygan, MI
1988

Roger Bennett
Camp Kingswood
Bridgton, ME
1990

The more interviews we held, the more we were staggered by the sheer breadth of impact the institution of camp has had on our generation. We began to understand that every camp is a unique compressed world with its own rhythm and traditions. Camp is also enhanced with more ritual than your average Shriner Temple. The variations between these worlds were vast, effectively making the choice of camp a life-changing decision. We interviewed former bunk mates from all-girls camps where the culture was pure and virginal. Boys were not seen and were rarely missed. Summers were spent mastering the harp, canoeing, and making jewelry. We also encountered bunk mates from another camp of the all-girls variety who spent their summer hanging out in the cabin, shacked up with a bong, treating every social as an opportunity for some Dana Plato–esque debauchery. All of the former ended up in publishing. All of the latter now work in the fashion industry.

The critical element that set summer camp apart from high school and college, and that shaped so many lives, is that it was expressly designed to make sure that everyone became part of a community, at a time when traditional pillars of community—clubs, places of worship, and even bowling leagues—were all in sharp decline. Well-defined hierarchies existed. The beautiful and the athletic shone. But if you had neat handwriting, were the king of the archery range, or played a mean piano, you could find your niche. Far away from everything that was familiar, each camper had little choice but to assimilate into this new social order, because camp was a place in which it was impossible to be alone.

Camp also offered everyone a second chance to start over and, freed from the shackles of their hometown reputations, be the kind of kid they always wanted to be. If you longed to be seen as a clotheshorse, a cutup, a ladies' man, or a dodgeball expert, here was your opportunity to reinvent yourself with confidence. The only constant was the predictability and repetition of the camp rituals, which served to reinforce the sense that the only thing that changed year to year was *you*.

Camp culture is a unique juxtaposition of opposites. A cross between *Fantasy Island* and *Lord of the Flies*. Periods of frantic excitement coexist with long bursts of calm hanging out; the thrill of endless love one night can be replaced by the numbing pain of being dumped the next; the freedom to test your boundaries can exist alongside an unshakeable homesickness; a bunk can be a place of both vicious exclusion and serious bonding. These factors created ever-changing storylines, comparable only to the daytime soap operas like *Days of Our Lives* and *General Hospital* that were compulsory viewing back in the real world—the only difference being that in the soap opera of camp, you were the star.

Camp Camp is the history of it all. A coming-of-age story of self-definition and exploration, of friendship and mentorship, and (not to sound too Erica Jong) sexual awakening and experimentation. Camp was the place many first kissed, got to third base, or cross-dressed. It is also a curious story of style. This was a place where everything depended on the duds you sported and on how many garments fifteen young girls could collectively stuff into one bunk. And it is also a cultural history. There are few finer prisms than the American summer camp through which to detect the emergence of rap music, the rise of the World Wrestling Federation, Nike Air, the waxing and waning of the hold *Saturday Night Live* had on our imaginations, or the scientific effect of adding a Rob Lowe poster to a bunk of ninth-grade girls.

We would be remiss if we failed to thank those who have made this book possible. First of all, the camp directors and staff who made the magic happen, motivated, more often than not, by the richness of their own experiences when they were campers. We are in awe of you all and the way you have dedicated your lives to shaping those of thousands of teenagers. Second, we would like to thank the inventors of the Kodak Disc Camera, for your technology is the engine that drove this train. We estimate your cameras were the weapon of choice for 95 percent of the thousands of photographs we received. The graininess and poor definition of your photographs are much missed and deeply mourned.

Finally, we want to thank all of you who took the time to send in your photographs, tell us your stories, and trust us with your memories. Camp was a place in which there were few secrets, everything was discussed, and almost everything was discovered, and the level of honesty and the reflection we encountered throughout the project made it a joy to undertake. It is a great honor to present your photographs and your words, unvarnished, unfiltered, and straight from the source, in the equivalent of one big camp yearbook, stuffed with romance and rejection, order and anarchy, music and style, down to the very last raging hormone.

Friendship, loyalty, and courage forever!

Roger Bennett
Jules Shell
New York City

P.S. If your camp is not in this book, we apologize. E-mail us your classic shots via our website, www.campcampbook.com. We would love to see them.

P.P.S. If this book makes you want to reconnect with long-lost campmates, go to the amazing www.campalumni.com and get the bunk back together.

Magic Bus

"I'm so nervous I just sit and smile
Your house is only another mile"
—The Who

Like Mormon pioneers striking out for Utah, every summer a mass exodus of campers left the familiarity and comfort of home. By plane, bus, and automobile they traveled. Their destination: the Great American Outdoors. While history may have precedents for demographic shifts of this size—Mao's Long March may come to mind—rarely did they happen annually, voluntarily, and with so much luggage.

The arrival at camp was an occasion fraught with emotion. The air was thick with nervous excitement. Veteran campers had lived for this moment, counting down ten months of dead time back in the real world until their return to camp, their happy place, gussied up with fresh paint. First-time campers wandered around disoriented, shell-shocked by sudden homesickness, amid the logistical nightmare of trunks and duffels that lay scattered on the ground. Everyone waited to be assigned a bunk, wondering about what might occur in the weeks of camp that lay ahead like so much blank canvas. All of this took place against a backdrop of mountains, countryside, and lake. Yet the phrase "at one with nature" could not have been more misapplied. Yes, the American child had left the city and the suburbs far behind, but heaping portions of mall culture had come with them in the baggage they carried and via the regular reinforcements that would follow (aka the "care package").

This is me and Drew Engelson leaving for camp. I'm sporting an Aca Joe sweatshirt and we are proudly posing by my parents' diesel Mercedes-Benz in the parking lot of the train station in Great Neck. I was psyched to leave. The thought of staying home never crossed my mind. We were ready for action.

Kevin Asch
Camp Takajo
Naples, ME
1986

I remember being recruited by the camp director in 1979. He came to Cleveland with his Super 8 reel projector and screen. I was terrified of being homesick. He made it clear that I should not be worried. That he would personally take care of me. I signed up. He then died before the summer began.

David Wain, Camp Modin, Belgrade, ME

You would plan your first-day outfit with excruciating deliberation in the week before camp started. The trick was to pick out the Esprit tank top and matching shorts that would make just the right statement. We flew into Portland airport. A bus drove us to camp through the towns of New England—Dresden, Maine; Poland, Maine; Vienna, Maine—all the places Jews had been expelled from in the old country. Now we were back.

The tradition was to be utterly silent on the bus once you arrived at the camp gates. We drove down the road and parked at the theater. It was totally thrilling. Our camp had a mile-long drive leading up to it. Tradition decreed that upon sight of the Walden sign there was great hushing. The convoy of buses would proceed up the mile-long drive to camp past the stables, riding fields, and tennis courts in total silence until we pulled to a halt. Seeing camp for the first time each summer was something done with awe. We all looked out of the windows, our heads filled with all that was to come. Unless it was your first summer, in which case it was terrifying.

Bunks were preassigned. As were beds. Your fate for the summer had already been sealed. The only thing you had control over was what quilt you had, so that became a big deal. You had to show your bona fides by bringing a down comforter, preferably made by Laura Ashley. There was a great sense of theater as you spread out that Lily of the Valley, and your pillowcase—my mom doused mine in her perfume, Calix, so I could smell her all summer. Tack your Michael Jackson photo over the bed by a shot of the family and your bed was ready for you to lie on and feel homesick.

Vanessa Kroll, Camp Walden, Denmark, ME

No matter how much you loved camp, the first night of the summer is always tough. One kid in your bunk is guaranteed to start crying and the rest of us would start sobbing. It didn't matter that you had not given your parents a second thought until then, homesickness is so contagious. All it took was that one kid and the rest of us fell like dominoes.

Mark Boxer, Camp Watitoh, Becket, MA

Getting on the bus to leave

The whole community came out to the departure point, a church parking lot in Little Neck. There were a lot of tears from the kids, and a lot of parents who were thinking about the freedom they were about to experience, and the European vacations they were about to embark upon. The buses began to pull out in convoy, but as they did, one stopped, bringing the whole lot to a halt. The doors opened in slow motion, and to my horror, my older daughter came down the steps in tears, carrying her luggage and begging not to go. The other parents' reaction was immediate. As my husband and I tried to reason with our daughter, a number of them came over and started swearing at us. "Throw her back on the bus. Let's get out of here, or my kid will be off the bus next and there goes the European vacation." I was caught between my kid and the community and forced to think quickly. We struck a deal. My daughter would get back on the bus, and my husband and I would follow her on the four-hour drive to camp in our car. And if she was still homesick when she arrived, we would drive her right home. She agreed to this. The convoy of buses resumed their journey, and with a mixture of relief and no small amount of guilt, my husband and I exited the parking lot and drove straight home.

Ellen Schweber, Camp Danbee, Hinsdale, MA
1978

Bye Dad!...   Bye Mom!...

Saying good-bye before going to camp. Me in knee-high white socks, my mom in an eighties hair helmet, and my father with his Harold Ramis haircut. My mother's shirt matches the *Miami Vice* logo on my cap, my prized possession.

Josh Frank, Echo Hill Ranch, Medina, TX
1985

June 27, 1983

Dear Mom,
Please pick me up from camp tomorrow. I'm so homesick. Bye. Please pick me up!

Love,

Katie Schumacher
French Woods
Hancock, NY
1983

Critical questions on the first day:
Who looks good? What bunk am I in?
Which girls are back?
Whose tits have grown?

David Light
Camp Ramah in the Poconos
Lake Como, PA

MONDAY,
JUNE 27, 1983

DEAR JENNA:

HI THERE SWEETIE PIE!!! WE HOPE THAT YOU HAD A NICE BUS TRIP UP TO CAMP AND ENJOYED THE SCENERY.

AS YOU CAN SEE IF YOU LOOK AT THE TOP OF THIS LETTER, I AM WRITING THIS LETTER TO YOU ON MONDAY, 4 DAYS BEFORE YOU EVEN LEFT FOR CAMP. I WANTED YOU TO HAVE A LETTER FROM US WHEN YOU ARRIVED IN CAMP.

WE HOPE YOU GET A NICE COMFORTABLE BED WITH NICE GIRLS SURROUNDING YOU. REMEMBER, DON'T BE UNCOMFORTABLE ABOUT MAKING NEW FRIENDS AND ALSO REMEMBER THAT EVERYONE FEELS A LITTLE STRANGE THE FIRST FEW DAYS BEING AWAY FROM HOME SO DON'T THINK THAT YOU ARE THE ONLY ONE FEELING THAT WAY. IF YOU ARE UPSET ABOUT SOMETHING, DON"T BE AFRAID TO TALK TO THE COUNSELLOR OR MIKE OR ROCHELLE ABOUT IT.

WE WILL BE THINKING ABOUT YOU ALL THE TIME AND HOPE THAT YOU HAVE A WONDERFUL, WONDERFUL, WONDERFUL TIME. DON'T FORGET TO WRITE TO US AND TELL US WHAT YOU ARE DOING.

WE LOVE YOU AND SEND FIVE THOUSAND HUGS AND KISSES TO YOU.

LOVE
XXXXOOOO
MOMMY & DADDY

Mary Quant ©

Jenna Fallon
Camp Edward Isaacs
Holmes, NY
1983

Henry Jacobs
Utica, MS
c. 1984

Pretty in Pink

"Caroline laughs and it's raining all day,
She loves to be one of the girls"
—The Psychedelic Furs

The girls' bunk was about who was IN and who was OUT. A vicious social hierarchy gelled as the bunks were organized and decorated. By the time storage bins were stuffed to the gills with Esprit and Fiorucci, the Jackie Collins and *Sweet Valley High* books had been neatly shelved, and the last Debbie Gibson poster was tacked onto the wall, the pecking order was in place, cementing who would be victim, perpetrator, and bystander for the rest of the summer. This hierarchy was determined by a complicated set of informal but widely known factors: Were you beautiful or physically advanced, and if so, could you carry your assets with confidence? Were you blessed with Navratilova-esque sports skill or a lock for the lead role in this season's musical? Failing all of the above, did you have an older sibling in camp, making you instantly cool because the older campers would say hello to you in the dining room?

Once the social order was determined, the bunk became a place of absolute truth. Any opinion, no matter how hurtful, could be voiced publicly, straight to another bunk mate's face, making the cabin a place of mental torture in which techniques befitting the CIA's PSYOPS manual were commonplace. If someone was excluded, their exclusion was total. Alliances shifted constantly, and the only thing you could trust was your hair dryer, apart from the hour before dinner when fuses would ritually blow. In this setting, the drama of the summer played out like an Edith Wharton novel recorded only in the graffiti that filled the walls by summer's end, preserving for posterity exactly who was a fine, upright citizen and who was an easy slut.

Jenna Fallon
Camp Edward Isaacs
Holmes, NY
1987

23

HOW TO MAKE FRIENDS AND INFLUENCE PEOPLE: THE POWER OF CAMP CALLIGRAPHY

In the world of the girls' bunk, there were many paths to popularity, but among the least appreciated by historians is the power and status afforded to the girl with the nice handwriting. Because summer camp is a temporary world and one in which an array of team lists, activity posters, and programs always needed to be made, sign-making was a constant task. Before the dawn of the technological revolution and the abundant font choices, clip art, and document templates that were among its most important inventions, having neat handwriting was the status equivalent of having a hot boyfriend or at least a really good wardrobe. Cool handwriting was a way to distinguish yourself from the rest of the group, but this skill did not come naturally. It was born from hours of constant practice in the run-up to summer in the three main esoteric forms of the art: the Dot letters, the Bubble font, and the most complex, the Rainbow. To this day, no one knows who invented them, but they became camp standard, and can still be admired on the sides of shower caddies, on *Baby-sitters Club* stationery, and on Splash books across the nation.

FROM ADAM
TO JULIE TO
SAM FROM
IE TO JULIE
M ADAM FRO
JULIE TO
FROM A DAN
TO JULIE T
FROM
TO J
FR

URRR SHURRR!

BANQUET
82

Ha-Ha don't rip the envelope, Julie.

J U L I E
Gimme a   Gimme a   Gimme a   Gimme a   Gimme a   ? what does it spell?   ● ← planet
                                                                                    _____
                                                                                    Fill In

This Great Letter Was Brought To You By
Jane

PLEASE SEND MY 2 PILLOWS, MY SLEEPING BAG, A TINY BOX OF POWDER, AND MY TEDDY BEAR - I'M REAL SORRY!

- IF ERIC DIDN'T TAKE THE LIGHT BLUE TOWEL

MOM - I HAVEN'T GOTTEN A LETTER IN 2 DAYS!!

WARNING: RE-READINGS OF THIS LETTER MAY BE HAZZARDOUS TO YOUR HEALTH, AND WILL PROBABLY CAUSE BRAIN DAMAGE. ANYONE WITHOUT A BRAIN, OF COURSE, HAVE NO FEAR.

WRITE SOON!

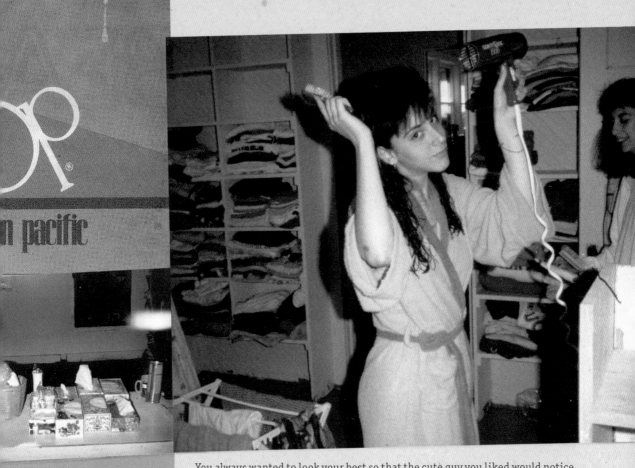

You always wanted to look your best so that the cute guy you liked would notice you, ask you to go on a walk after dinner, hook up with you later in a vacant guest cabin, and ultimately profess his love to you by writing you a note inscribed with the lyrics of the bridge from "Every Breath You Take."

Sarah Sokolic, Camp Ramah in the Berkshires, Wingdale, NY
1988

Every summer at Camp Thunderbird all the girls came prepared "just in case" they started menstruating. Always (with wings) were a big hit one particular summer. I was hiding in my cabin with a friend, skipping out on our assigned activities, when we found somebody's ginormous box of winged maxi pads. In a moment of genius, we took out a pad and in red Sharpie I wrote, "Sara this is your period speaking to you." We then placed the maxi pad into a pair of Sara Gordon's white cotton undies and placed them crotch-up in her cubby.

Julia Wolov, Camp Thunderbird, Bemidji, MN

We were CIT's that year and spent the entire time at camp in the beautiful backwoods of Michigan beautifying ourselves as if we were in the city.

Debbie Shell
Camp Walden
Cheboygan, MI
1988

As the oldest female cabin, we thought the face masks at breakfast made us seem mature. We loved the attention we got in the dining hall.

Emily Selden, YMCA of Greater Des Moines Y Camp, Boone, IA
1989

Kate Lee
Camp Eisner
Great Barrington, MA
1991

This was from my first summer at
Tripp Lake. I remember being very
excited to get the only bunk bed.
I was even more excited to put up
the metal mouth poster I got from
my orthodontist. I thought it was
cool when I was twelve.

Georgia Liebman
Tripp Lake Camp, Poland, ME
1990

The cubby of Beth Landis. Beth had the best clothes and the neatest cubby. We were in awe of her.

Sarah Sokolic
Camp Ramah in the Berkshires, Wingdale, NY
1987

Jaime was incredibly talented. The entire cabin would go crazy for her being able to blow her nose with her feet, and we would encourage her to do so during cleanup.

Marci Sukenic
Camp Walden, Cheboygan, MI
1987

Jacobs Camp
Utica, MS
1987

IT'S A HARD KNOCK LIFE

BY MOLLY ROSEN

A ll I ever wanted was to be cool. I idolized my big sister. Her bushy hair. Her Huey Lewis and the News rhinestone pin and her Magic-Markered mix-tape covers, her layered black and pink scrunch socks and her Stage Three areolas. I was nerdy and pale. I had blue braces and blue glasses and one corn-kernel nipple. Don't ask about the other one. I liked Patrick Swayze and Inspector Gadget and lox. I longed to grow up, to find my wild side.

But my big sister Becca was too busy to mentor me, so I needed to find surrogates. The solution bolted up my back over a rice-and-beans family dinner like electroshock. My sister had been a devout camper for years and had regaled me with great tales of canoe trips and making fun of fat girls with headgear. I realized, in a flash, that I needed to replicate this experience and go to summer camp to study the older girls. There, among an erotic landscape of blueberry pancakes and pine perfume, I would learn to French inhale, have abortions, and do complicated dances with damaged men in the lake. I quickly became obsessed with every camp in the Great Lakes area. I watched every promotional video every day after school, right after watching my favorite taped episode of *Family Ties,* the one where Jennifer got busted for hosting a beer party behind Elyse's and Steven's backs. In the videos, girls romped around wooded hills and made lanyards while John Denver sang about West Virginia. They wore long T-shirts and seemed in on the secrets I, too, wanted to know. I settled on Birch Trail in Minong, Wisconsin. The camp's video gave me the sense it contained plenty of ne'er-do-well suburbanites eager to corrupt me with Kool cigarettes, Lee Press-on Nails, thick wads of rubber bracelets running up their forearms, and Harlequin Romance–worthy tales of getting to third base with skateboarders and Robert Smith.

It took one day at Birch Trail for me to realize this was not to be the case. My counselors were portly girls with side ponytails who played "Moonshadow" by Cat Stevens on repeat as we unpacked our bags. They were not a paragon of cool like my sister. Rather than resembling Jennifer's hip friends on *Family Ties,* they looked more like the kind of women who would date Dudley on *Diff'rent Strokes.* My bunk mates were hairless and newtlike. Their names were Polly and Lucille and Muffy and they brought with them no makeup and only one bottle of pink Pert shampoo. From within the inner folds of their monogrammed bags emerged grapefruit vagina spray, peachy armpit spray, and rosy powder for their preteen Camembert labia. They paid no attention to my temporary black hair dye, or my provocative announcement that I had once given a hand job to a Korean man named Jake Ryan on a trip to Niagara Falls. The worst was yet to come. Before dinner, Side Pony Number One emerged from behind her tapestry with a banjo and a triumphant announcement: According to camp tradition, our cabin was to be called the Upper Maples.

We filed into the mess hall. I looked hopefully for the rebels. There they were, sitting like sisters at a long table in the back of the dining hall. A buzzing cocoon of crinkly perms, heaving breasts, heavy earrings. My heroes. A girl with a jiggly cantaloupe ass and Umbros stood defiantly atop a chair and belted an ironic line from *Yentl.* Her adoring onlookers hooted and high-fived. I pictured their Stage Five pubic patches growing proud pea shoots and curly jungles beneath their palmetto short shorts. My own neglected mons was still bald as a baseball. All of a sudden, my calling in life became clear as a crystal: all I needed to become complete was to be accepted into their pubic-hair tribe. "Those are the Tamaracks," said a fellow Newt. "I can't wait until I can be one. It will only take five years."

A corpulent man named Stan with a beard and a pair of turquoise Jams stood at the microphone. He was the camp director. He wore water socks and a shit-eating grin. His wife, Bobby, wore Tretorns and a dinosaur T-shirt. She stood by his side beaming as he opened proceedings with the camp's

Molly Rosen
Birch Trail Camp for Girls
Minong, WI
1987

signature welcome. "How, campers, how!" All the girls obediently replied in unison.

"Welcome back, ladies. I know in previous years, we have sung with gusto in the name of good, clean fun. But Bobby and I have attended many a conference this winter, and we have learned that that kind of rabble-rousing behavior promotes anorexia among our youth. So do us all a favor and let us all refrain from that age-old Birch Trail tradition. In the name of health!"

"HOW!" Cantaloupe Ass snorted. I tried desperately to make eye contact with her, even going so far as to waggle my spirit fingers in her direction with hope in my heart that she might storm over to me and teach me a secret handshake, forever cementing our solidarity and sisterhood. No such luck. She never even looked in my direction. I waggled my fingers harder toward a pretend fly circling around my hair. Her breasts were at Stage Four. A tear slid down the inside of my aorta.

Week One. After singing my eyes out during the audition, I am cast as Miss Hannigan in *Annie.* My delight is short-lived when I learn that the Tamaracks do their own play, an awesome rendition of *Oliver!* that us Maples are excluded from. Does that mean they are similarly excluded from our performance, meaning Cantaloupe Ass won't be there to witness my deft, scene-stealing performance? I learn to tie-dye a pillowcase.

Week Two. Shaman, a jack-of-all-trades who watches the waterfront with a smear of zinc oxide on his nose, takes our bunk into the woods for an afternoon of trust-building exercises. An endomorph with an acid-washed fanny pack stands on a log and trembles for forty-five whole minutes while we make a nest with our arms behind her. Shaman loses it and starts yelling, I make erotic eye contact with him, and Lindsey Leigh, a Dallas vixen who is eleven, sprays an entire bottle of Salon Selectives hairspray into the air in an act of protest. Side Pony Number Two catches her, starts to cry, and says the ozone is going to disintegrate and she is going to get fired. I tie-dye all my hankies.

Week Three. We go into town. I buy suede-fringed Minnetonka moccasin ankle boots. They are the same shoes that Cantaloupe Ass has. I learn that her name is Dana. She is Oliver in the Tamarack play. All the boys surround her at every social as soon as she descends from the bus in her scrunch socks. Her voice is deep and her legs are bowed and her hair is bright blond. Her younger sister is named Lucille Bernstein and she is in my bunk. I hate Lucille. She's a redhead and her areolas are inverted. Once she put a goldfish cracker on her flashlight after lights-out and giggled for five minutes about the large shadow it made on the ceiling like it was the wildest thing a woman has ever done.

Yesterday during free time I wrote "red pubic hair" on Lucille's hairbrush in pink nail polish in the secret hopes that Dana might hate Lucille, too, want to know who defiled her horrible sister's possessions, and take me under her wing. No such luck. Lucille cried to Dana, Dana yelled at me, and now all the Tamaracks officially hate my guts. I tie-dye every T-shirt I brought with me.

Week Four. I am going home on Sunday. My play is tomorrow. My parents called the camp to see if they could drive up and watch my moment of glory but Stan said Birch Trail is a sacred space and any disruption from the outside world is upsetting to the youth. I hate Lucille more and more. I blame her for everything including Mary's blindness on *Little House on the Prairie.* My worst-case scenario came true. Although the Tamaracks were not excluded from our performance of *Annie,* not one bothered to show up for my crowning glory. I was predictably devastated and in a desperate last-minute bid for attention, chose the last night's campfire and a sing-along as a stage from which to regale my fellow Newt campers with tales of my sexual escapades. The reptile penis I once fellated in the projects of Cabrini-Green. The ballsac I cupped in my palm while fending off a mugger in my public school playground. I am eleven years old. I have never kissed a boy. But my older sister Becca's collection of V. C. Andrews books have muddled my mind with enough incest and insanity to last a lifetime. I talked loudly in the hopes Dana might stop by my storytelling session, realize I was secretly in need of a hug, and drop everything to sweep me up in her blond embrace. But she was too busy French-braiding Lucille's red hair, singing "Leaving on a Jet Plane," and writing down her wishes for the year, throwing them in the fire, and beating her bosom while she wept. The morning before I leave, I tie-dye my sheets, shorts, socks, and scrunchies in a fit of rage and frustration.

I then returned to Chicago and quickly became a different girl. The corn kernel became a gently steamed patty pan squash. The other breast blossomed into a tender frozen pea. A faint downy cobweb of pubic hair emerged one day like a miracle. I discovered *Interview* magazine and Axl Rose. Doc Martens boots. Mood rings. Janis Joplin. Baileys. Black lights. Spin the bottle. That you could pierce your ears three times with the same safety pin and shred holes in your jeans with a simple set of scissors. Sun-In and a straightening iron flattened any fear I had of a Jewfro. Stan and Bobby materialized in a hotel conference room for a reunion wearing winter coats some months later. My hair was bright blond and bone straight. I looked like Hitler's honey. Pocket T's were in that year, perfect for concealing my smaller breast beautifully. This summer, I would be a Lower Linden. My Minnetonkas were worn just right. I had successfully tie-dyed every item of white clothing in our house, including my father's business shirts, which I belted and wore with my cleaning lady Carla's rosaries. I left the reunion with Birch Trail's latest promotional video in hand. To my sheer delight, three seconds of my Miss Hannigan debut had made it onto film. I ran home from school every night to watch it on repeat, after a taped television-friendly version of *The Breakfast Club.* I now had a role in history. I mattered. I meant something. One day I was certain to be a star.

Molly Rosen
Birch Trail Camp for Girls
Minong, WI
1988

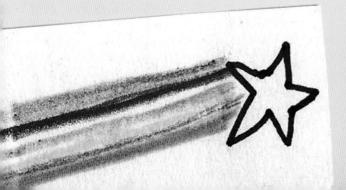

Everything was traded, clothes-wise. Especially the wide array of colored Champion sweatshirts.

"We're wearing Champions this year. The 'C' on our sweatshirts is so clear. You're not my friend if you don't wear a Champion . . ."

Jackie Kristel
Camp Merriwood, Orford, NH

Lisa Wainer
Camp Walden, Cheboygan, MI
1991

We had these T's made up for ourselves at a custom shop on a day trip to Cape Cod. KA3H was the name we came up for ourselves—Karen, Karin, Carrie, and Heidi—three *K*'s and an *H*. Carrie got short-changed a little, but she did not complain.

Karen Lauterstein
KenWood Camp, Kent, CT
1986

When I first arrived at camp I found myself in the loser bunk. I was a late bloomer and still kind of a dorky tomboy. The official camp outfit was tan and green and white. My mother was the only one who sent me away with exact specifications. Everyone else had stylistically evolved to Dolphin and Izod. My hair was short and everyone—everyone—else's was feathered. I had never used a hair dryer in my life and so had no idea what to do with myself during rest hour—tribe time—when everyone spent hours feathering their hair or walking around the lower ball fields to make out. I was from the rougher urban set of Brooklyn. Everyone else was from New Jersey and Long Island. Camp was like my crash course in suburban living, which revolved around music, sports, and kissing.

Amy Israel, Camp Watitoh, Becket, MA

Camp was in the middle of nowhere. We did not care how we looked, what clothes we wore, how we looked in a bathing suit. No one ever wore makeup. Or showered enough. Weight and looks became irrelevant. Camp was a dirty place—it was about fishing, canoeing, and hiking. It was a place where you could just be. One summer the camp director came round to my bunk on the last day with a hairbrush. I had not brushed my hair all summer.

Katie Rosman, Camp Thunderbird, Bemidji, MN

Getting ready for a bunk photo or our first Grateful Dead show—you choose. While some of these shirts were custom-made in creative arts, others were purchased for $50 at a boutique in Scarsdale or Long Island.

Lori Harrison
Camp Romaca, Hinsdale, MA
1991

The summer going into eighth grade—the awkward summer. Although activities were provided, much of the day was spent lounging around in bed, eating snacks, and reading magazines. *Beverly Hills, 90210* was the rage and the wall is covered with pictures of Luke Perry and Shannen Doherty. They are on the cover of *YM* magazine, too. We just couldn't get enough and it was totally acceptable to be equally obsessed with both male and female celebrities.

Ilana Kunstanowitz, Camp Ramah in the Berkshires, Wingdale, NY
1991

At lights-out our drunk counselors would come in and tell us all about their lives. We would discuss critical questions of the day such as: "If your partner could know everything you were thinking, would you want that?" I would lie there thinking whether that was possible.

Sloane Crosley, Camp Wa-klo, Keane, NH

All you do in this all-girls world is talk about boys. Our knowledge and our expertise grew every year. When you are younger you just go along, pretending that you know more and that you have done more. In the last years of camp, the proportion flips, and actually doing stuff with boys as opposed to just talking about it takes over to the extent that you would ruin your friendships with even your best friends over a boy.

Ariel Silberman, Camp Echo Lark, Poyntelle, PA

Boom boxes and Walkmen were strictly forbidden at our camp. One girl—Nicole—got a letter from her doctor saying she needed a Walkman on medical grounds to get to sleep. More than anything I missed TV. *Saved by the Bell. The Cosby Show.* We spent the whole summer talking about television. I was blown away the first time I discovered that what was Fox 5 in New York was Channel 29 in Connecticut.

Anonymous, Tripp Lake Camp, Poland, ME

I learned women can be venal and mean and superficial, but when you connect, those bonds are priceless . . . whispered conversations about the most intimate subjects in the world in the darkness of the bunk. Camp was like church to me, it was so profound.

Lauren Sandler, Camp Wyonegonic, Denmark, ME

**Lauren Senderoff
Camp Echo Lark, Poyntelle, PA
1987**

One of our counselors suggested that we put on our swimsuits, wrap towels around ourselves, take our straps off
our shoulders and hide them under the towels, and pose
like we'd just been caught coming from the showers or
KYBOs (which stands for Keep Your Bowels Open).

Claire Zulkey, Camp Echo, Fremont, MI
1991

GILLIAN LAUB: HOUSE OF STYLE

Although the lakes of Maine and the rivers of Wisconsin are about as far from the catwalks of gay Paris as one can travel, at many camps it seemed as if Madison Avenue were just around the corner. The brands rarely seemed to change: Esprit, Camp Beverly Hills, or EG's, as well as the camp equivalent of the little black dress—the Champion sweatshirt. A numbing of taste led to the tie-dyeing of everything. But what set the truly stylish apart was less the clothes and more that je ne sais quoi of confidence, ripeness, and poise. To that end, we salute Gillian Laub of Trail's End Camp, whose depth of wardrobe and overall sassiness meant that if there were to be a Nobel Prize for accessorizing, she would win it hands down.

THE PURITY TEST

MOS = MEMBER OF THE OPPOSITE SEX

HAVE YOU EVER...?

1) had a date
2) been on a date past 4:00 a.m.
3) had a blind date
4) kissed an MOS
5) been French kissed
6) kissed an MOS in a horizontal position
7) French kissed three (3) or more MOS's in twenty-four (24) hours
8) kissed an MOS in last three (3) months
9) necked for more than two (2) hours consecutively
10) slow danced cheek to cheek
11) had an alcoholic drink (holidays and religious festivals do not count)
12) been drunk
13) driven drunk or on drugs
14) had a lapse of memory due to drugs or alcohol
15) used alcoholic drinks to lower an MOS's resistance
16) smoked tobacco
17) smoked pot or hashish
18) used a stronger drug
19) taken four (4) or more different recreational drugs in one (1) night
20) read a pornographic book or magazine
21) seen a pornographic movie
22) seen a stripper
23) been arrested
24) been convicted of a crime
25) had an erection or clitoral erection
26) had an orgasm
27) had an orgasm in a dream
28) fondled an MOS's butt
29) caressed an MOS's thigh
30) fondled a girl's breasts or had breasts fondled
31) wrestled with an MOS
32) showered, bathed, jacuzzied, etc. nude with an MOS
33) gone skinny dipping
34) gone through motions of intercourse while fully dressed
35) spent the night in an MOS's bedroom
36) slept in the same bed with an MOS
37) seen a post-pubescent nude
38) been seen nude by an MOS after puberty
39) undressed or been undressed by an MOS
40) kissed breasts of an MOS or had breasts kissed
41) fondled an MOS's genitals or had genitals fondled
42) had orgasm due to manipulation by an MOS
43) kissed an MOS on the thigh
44) engaged in cunnilingus
45) engaged in fellatio   oral sex
46) gone sixty-nine (69)
47) engaged in definite sexual behavior on first date
48) masturbated
49) masturbated to a picture
50) masturbated with another person in the room
51) been caught masturbating
52) watch someone else masturbate

53) committed an act of exhibitionism
54) committed an act of voyeurism
55) simulated intercourse with an inanimate object
56) massaged or been massaged by an MOS
57) unintentionally interrupted a couple in a state of undress
58) participated in a tickle-orgy, gross out, truth or dare, or similar activity
59) experimented sexually before puberty
60) had intercourse
61) purchased contraceptives in a drug store
62) had sex more than ten (10) times ever
63) had continuous sex for more than a half hour
64) had sex in last three (3) months
65) had sex three (3) or more times in one (1) night
66) had sex in more than three (3) positions
67) had sex in a car
68) had sex using a condom
69) had sex at a house when the parents are home
70) had sex outdoors
71) had sex with three (3) different people seperately
72) had sex with a virgin
73) had sex during menstruation or with a girl during her menstrual period
74) had sex without birth control
75) had sex with two (2) MOS's in twenty-four (24) hours
76) described a sexual experience you had with an MOS to another person
77) committed statutory rape
78) traveled one hundred (100) miles or more for sex
79) impregnated a woman or been pregnant
80) arranged or had an abortion
81) displaced a roommate by sleeping overnight with an MOS one (1) or more nights
82) shacked up with an MOS for one (1) month or more
83) tasted semen
84) been propositioned by a pimp or prostitute
85) accepted
86) had anal intercourse
87) had a VD test due to a reasonable suspicion
88) picked up a strange MOS for sexual enjoyment
89) engaged in group sex
90) engaged in satism or masochism
91) been propositioned by a homosexual
92) accepted
93) been masturbated by a member of the same sex
94) been orally stimulated by a member of the same sex
95) committed incest
96) engaged in transvestism for sexual enjoyment
97) committed rape or been raped
98) fondled a pre-pubescent
99) committed beastiality

The Purity Test. We would take this at the beginning of camp and then over and over again all the way through the summer. Your score would start at a virginal 83 and steadily plummet to the low sixties. In the still of night after a social, we would compare notes about how many points we had lost the night before.

Rachel Cohen, Camp Tel Yehudah
Barryville, NY
1985

Every summer we would take professional photos at Timber Ridge. Timber Ridge All Stars was the background for the photos. We got to pick the sport. In other years I picked tennis. This year I was too cool to pick a sport. The sweatshirt is Swatch— I borrowed it and loved it.

Gabbi Robinson, Timber Ridge, Highview, WV
1986

Walking down the path from the bunks. Camp was important for me. It was where I learned that boys are fun to kiss.

Dany Levy, Camp Laurel, Readfield, ME
1984

Heidi Lender
Camp Tapawingo, Sweden, ME
1977

To stop little girls from arguing about superficial issues, we were forced to wear a uniform. Green-and-white T-shirts. We hated the uniform. But girls always find a way to compete. Some girls got their swimsuits from J. Crew and L.L. Bean. We had this one girl whose father owned a liquor company and another who was essentially Spanish royalty—it looked like they may have commissioned Missoni to make theirs, or else they wore green polyester like Claudia Schiffer. I got mine at the camp-recommended Army & Navy supply store until I wised up and started ordering solid green suits from J. Crew. They made one that was forest green with white straps and white piping that I loved.

Sloane Crosley, Camp Wa-Klo, Keane, NH
1989

Sara Solfanelli
Camp Tegawitha
Tobyhanna, PA
1989

Lochearn Camp staff donning our "Sunday Campfire" outfits. It was a Scottish camp, so the outfit included a "plaid." And, if you were the cabin in charge of the campfire program for the week, you also wore a little blue bonnet.

Julie Jacobs, Camp Lochearn, Post Mills, VT
1983

BOYS' BUNK

Bad Boys

"Run on off to school
Your child your man grows up a fool"
—Wham!

Going to sleep in the boys' bunk was a fatal mistake. You could wake up in the middle of the lake with your bed balanced on kayaks, or be induced into the act of wetting yourself by having your hands dipped in a bucket of water. The combination of the fear of humiliation and the spirit of one-upmanship meant that by the end of summer nighttime was panic-inducing. Bunk mates forced themselves to stay awake through the night, determined not to be *that* guy who woke up with his face covered in shaving cream, or worse.

In the daylight hours, the boys' side of camp was a primitive place in which the sound of playing cards being shuffled and dealt filled the air. Bare-chested and proud, campers often looked ready for a casting call for *Stand by Me.* They would have barely unpacked before descending into a testosterone-fueled world of competitive wrestling, weight lifting, towel whipping, and boner comparison, all designed to separate the men from the boys.

But the boys' bunk was also a place of radical inclusion. Amid the peculiar stench of wet towels, Deep Heat, Hai Karate aftershave, and pine sap that hung heavily, there was much that brought the bunkmates together. A stash of communal porn hidden in the rafters was one example. Used medicinally, like an iron lung, the stash was guaranteed to have something for every budding fetish, from *Girls with Guns* to *Big Butts*. For the more anthropologically inclined, there were also several copies of *National Geographic.* The freedom of the camp experience, and the immense amount of time spent just hanging out, meant that the friendships forged in this veritable Fagin's den would last for a lifetime, though, thanks to the science of nicknaming, none of your new friends called you by your real name.

Kevin Harrison
Camp Sequoia
Rock Hill, NY
1983

20 ACTS OF VIOLENCE THAT SAY "I LOVE YOU"

Adam Goldberg
Camp Echo Lark, Poyntelle, PA
1987

In the days before Judge Judy was a national TV star and America became an overly litigious society, the boys' bunk was like a peewee Abu Ghraib where torture was standard operating procedure. This list of random acts of violence may make you wince, but it is important to note that many of the campers who were victims of every-day sadism actually loved it. In the words of one, "To be on the wrong end of a rattail or an atomic wedgie meant that the counselor noticed you—that in a perverse way, you had arrived." So remember that, dear reader, as you peruse the list. Settle back, relax, and marvel at the detail and creativity that went into some of these acts. The elaborate flourishes—especially the use of toothpaste or deodorant to maximize the pain—stand as a unique tribute to the innovative spirit that made this country great.

1. The Reverse Wedgie

A variation on the classic attack. Underpants are ripped upward but point of attack is from the front.
Common act, multiple camps

2. Atomic Wedgie

You would pull up the waistband of the underpants until it rips and then place it over the victim's head like a chin strap.

David Light, Camp Ramah in the Poconos,
Lake Como, PA

3. Bungee Wedgie

Wedgie executed at the end of a bungee cord hung from the rafters of a boys' cabin. "Once hung by his tighty-whities a boy was then batted around the cabin by the other boys on the ground below him. Think Cirque du Soleil . . . This hurt so much that we would pre-rip our underpants so that the whole ordeal did not last too long."

David Greenbaum, Camp Chingachgook,
Lake George, NY

4. Skyhook Wedgie (aka the Hook of Death)

Camper was left to hang by his white underpants on a nail until they tore in a kind of camp crucifixion.

Jake Sussman, Camp Moosilauke, Orford, NH

5. The Atomic Sit-Up

This elaborate trick involved a mark and a con. The victim would be informed you have invented a new kind of sit-up that is so relaxing it makes you feel great. A towel would then be placed over the dupe's face. The fattest kid in the bunk would then be brought into the mix. He would take down his shorts and put his ass right above the dupe's face. The dupe would then be commanded to do a sit-up. If the fat kid was really talented, he could time it to cut a fart right when the dupe sat up. That was the atomic bit.

Doug Grad, Tyler Hill Camp, Wayne, PA

6. Pink Belly (aka Hot Dog)

Hold a guy down. Slap his belly till it goes bright red. Schmear toothpaste on it for that extra sting.

Doug Herzog, Camp Scatico, Elizaville, NY

7. The Swirly

Place a camper's head in toilet and then flush it.

Simmy Kunstawitz, Camp Ramah in the Berkshires
Wingdale, NY

8. The Waffle Butt

A counselor takes a tennis racquet, whacks it against a kid's butt until it looks like a waffle. Repeat till bleeding. Spray Right Guard on bleeding wounds to maximize sting.

Common act, multiple camps

9. Trucking a Kid

Wait till victim is asleep. Shine flashlight at either side of head. Yell "TRUCK" to wake him. He would freak out, thinking he was in the middle of the highway. A variation was that someone would wear white sheets and talk to him in a deep voice and make him believe he was in the afterlife.

Common act, multiple camps

10. The Gas Pedal

Camper's legs are pulled apart as counselor stamps on his crotch area while exclaiming "Gas Pedal!"

Anonymous, Camp Cedar, Casco, ME

11. Teabagging

Counselor dipping testicles in the open mouth of sleeping camper or at least resting them on the eye sockets. The homoeroticism never factored in for the person doing the dipping.

Common act, multiple camps

12. Rattails

We had one counselor, Larry, who looked like Sergeant Slaughter. He wound his towel so tight, and wet, you had to put on an extra blanket to protect yourself. But you wanted him to hit you, show you that he cared about you . . . he had noticed you.

Alex Goodman, Camp Cedar, Casco, ME

13. Brown Round

Take hot rubbing sauce we used to buy in the mall (there was hot, extra hot, and WOW!—guess which we used?) and rub on a kid's lips while he is sleeping.

Brad Feldman, Camp Greylock, Becket, MA

14. The Bladder Burst

Place sleeping camper's hand in a bowl of warm water. Guaranteed to make you wet the bed.

Common act, multiple camps

15. The Pile-on

Sleeping camper is woken by seven or more campers jumping on him, crushing him under cumulative weight. First camper on takes one for the team.

Common act, multiple camps

16. Bollocksing

Sleeping camper is woken up by counselor jabbing lacrosse stick up his ass cheeks. Lacrosse stick inserted in "a loving way, though, not one of those high school hazing ways."

Mitchell Whiteman, Lake Forest, Oakland, ME

17. Dead Arm

Knuckle punch to the meaty part of the arm muscle, which would turn camper's arm into one inflated bruise by the end of the summer.

Common act, multiple camps

18. Purple Nurple

A newfangled name for the old-fashioned titty twist. A variation was the Munching Cow Bite, which became the Shark Bite after *Jaws* the movie came out—reaching into the inner thigh and squeezing hard.

Michael Solomon, Camp Androscoggin, Wayne, ME

19. Punch for Punch (aka Chest Shot)

You would stand opposite each other an arm apart and punch each other in the chest repeatedly. I fought a counselor once. And he destroyed me from the outset. My body was covered in bruises that were replicas of his fist. I could feel the internal bleeding. But I refused to give in. Because this game was all about being a man.

Adam Goldberg, Camp Echo Lark, Poyntelle, PA

20. Double Dump

We would take a dump and portion it out into two cups. One would be positioned under the bed and the other placed up in the rafters. Your bunk would stink. The victim would look under the bed, find one cup, and think they had solved the mystery. But the cup in the rafters would go on stinking for days.

Andrew Goldberg, Camp Wildwood, Bridgton, ME

This shot was taken immediately after my swim test at Camp Walden. I swear, even to this day, I have to convince my friends that this priceless green-and-black Speedo is indeed a swimsuit and *not* underwear.

Quote: Jason Boschan; Photo: Eric Michaels; Camp Walden, Cheboygan, MI 1989

I was a chronic bed wetter until the age of nine. Experience taught me two things: to never admit I wet the bed and to get the sheets out of the way as soon as possible. The trouble was that clean bedsheets don't just grow from the rafters. So the trick was to dramatically spill something like Kool-Aid on your sheets as early, and as visibly, as possible. This should be followed by a quick balling up of the sheets and a loud public announcement to your counselor that you would personally take care of making sure they got to the laundry, and before exiting the bunk with sheets, coolly laughing to yourself, "Kool-Aid! On the sheets again!!!"

Perry Silver, Falling Creek Camp, Tuxedo, NC

I moved to New York from London when I was eight, by which time everyone had been at camp for a couple of years. The first time I got to camp, I arrived a day late. Which was typical—my mum always got dates wrong. (She went to camp to surprise my twin sisters on their birthday once and turned up the day after—a day that was meant to be magic turned into a sulkfest.) I got there, and with my fear of heights, found all the lower bunks were taken. I was afraid of complaining and being forever known as a pussy, so I just swallowed it. I remember going to bed the first time and waking up in the middle of the night just in time for everything to go black as I hit the ground. My new bunk mates woke up to find me a broken mess on the floor. The camp doctor, a large jovial black man called Butch, sent me right to the hospital, proudly telling me, "We don't fuck around with head injuries, son."

Mark Ronson, Camp Amherst, Amherst, MA

Andrew Strickman
Camp Perlman
Starlight, PA
1986

Boys' camp can be tortuous if you have any kind of deformity like an indented chest. If your name was Kadushin, you were doomed to be called "douchebag" for eight weeks. No one would call you by your real name. No one would even remember it. Everyone had weird nicknames. Some made sense. Jeffrey Nelson had a big head. So he became Jeff Big Head. Some did not. Ziti got his name because at dinner someone just happened to call him that.

Andrew Goldberg, Camp Wildwood, Bridgton, ME

I had my first overnight camping experience at camp—the cookouts we had were formative.

Josh Bernstein
Camp Winaukee
Moultonboro, NH
1979

I am the one in the pink neck scarf. Let the record show, I was dressing like that pre-Wham.

Michael Solomon
Camp Androscoggin
Wayne, ME
1982

GARY'S LAST LAUGH

BY ADAM GOLDBERG

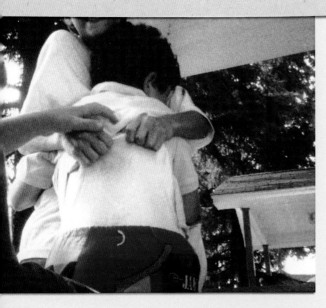

School was a nightmare of epic proportions. I was chubby and awkward and the perpetual best friend to every girl in the grade. I got beat up on the bus, I wore big glasses to correct my lazy eye, and I was so bad at sports, I once accidentally scored on my own goal during a hockey game. Life was about convincing people that I wasn't a geek, just a class clown with a big personality.

And then summer arrived and everything changed. I went to an enigma known as Jewish sports camp, a safe haven where everyone was just like me—geeky and awkward and picked last in gym class. The social hierarchy was reinvented and it was easy to reign at the top. I was suddenly the Jewish Wayne Gretzky and girls would actually French me at the Saturday night social. Gone was my nosy neurotic mother. Instead, I was "parented" by lazy, utterly irresponsible teenage counselors who would teach me about sex and give me a skyhook wedgie if I was out of line. Finally, my bunk mates and I were on our own. We were popular. We were athletic. And that meant we could be the bullies.

The target of our school-year-long pent-up aggression was fellow camper Gary Gersh. Every camp has one: that oddball kid who gets tortured relentlessly, but for some strange reason comes back year after year. Gary was shy, freckle-faced, with a wild, unkempt Jewfro. He was a camp legend. Once during an overnight camping trip, Gary had to go to the bathroom, dropped his Jams shorts, and squeezed out a giant turd right next to the campfire. We all looked on, mouths agape, marshmallows burning.

Gary saw it all. He got his mattress thrown out the window during a rainstorm. He got duct-taped into the shower stall for an hour. He got covered in mousse and shampoo as he slept. In the mess hall, the counselors would dunk his face in jelly and then start a chant for everyone to look at him. One time, a letter from his mother was intercepted and replaced with a fake letter saying that Grandma had been hit by a blimp. The poor kid believed it. His one great joy was listening to baseball on his AM-only radio, which my bunk mates constantly thwarted by stealing his batteries and throwing them in the toilet.

Adam Goldberg
(center)
Camp Echo Lark
Poyntelle, PA
1987

After four summers of torture, Gary finally started fighting back. His catchphrase became "SUCK MY WANG!" But even this backfired. One camper replied, "Okay, Gary. When we get back to the bunk, whip it out. If you have the guts." And so Gary marched right into our bunk and pulled out his junk for all to see. Unfortunately, some of my bunk mates were armed with cameras and were going to snap pictures to commemorate the humiliating occasion.

But the joke was on us. While we were all completely bald down there, it turned out Gary was a full-fledged MAN. Staring back at us was a girthy trouser monster rooted in a forest of thick, manly hair. Even in our alternate camp universe where we called the shots, our reliable dork had humbled us. Puberty had spoken. Loudly, and with lots of hair. The teasing died down after that day.

The summer ended and we returned home to resume our miserable geeky existences, where we'd count the days until we were the jocks and bullies again. I just hoped that next summer I wouldn't become the new Gary Gersh.

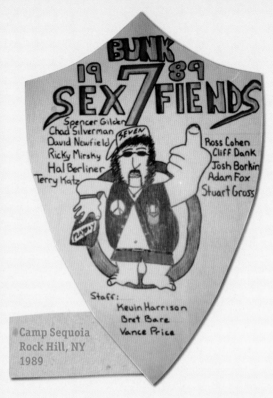

Camp Sequoia
Rock Hill, NY
1989

Tom Rosenberg
Camp Scatico, Elizaville, NY
1976

Boner contests were big features of our summer. Who had the biggest one? Forty of us would get warmed up, and then get together and throw down. All of a sudden Scott H. would pull his drawers off. No contest. He won every year. His nickname was Lube.

Ross Martin, Camp Harlam, Kresgeville, PA

We were very open in our bunk. First times were always up for discussion. We were all trying, and we all knew it. Success and failure could all be debated in an atmosphere of frank exchange. It was all for the common good. We couldn't wait for kids to get back to the bunk from a raid after we had all discussed what base we were trying for and with whom. Did he succeed or not? And as you listened to them report in, the sense of pressure was immense. Especially if he was not as cool as you and had gotten to a more advanced base. The whole thing was a massive collective experiment and a respectful competition at the same time.

Mark Boxer, Camp Watitoh, Becket, MA

It's amazing how one moment in camp can make you a legend. His name was Benny. He was just sitting on his bed, minding his own business. His bunk mate had just gotten out of the shower and was wagging his junk in Benny's face as a joke. And then it happened. Someone pushed Benny from behind and he fell forward, his mouth landing clean on his bunk mate's wang. Word spread like wildfire. Within hours he had the nickname Ball Sucker Benny. He left camp after only a week, but he was talked about for years to come.

Adam Goldberg, Camp Echo Lark, Poyntelle, PA

When I turned thirteen, I had my first wet dream. This was something of a mystery—I really couldn't put two and two together, because it was not preceded by any kind of sexual fantasy. Unless you count a big battle between Transformers and GoBots as such. There was a real dislocation between the physical me and the sexual me. But this was happening to a lot of us—aged eleven and twelve, we fought to stay up all night. Aged thirteen, we all wanted nothing more than to go to bed and enter that adolescent masturbatory world of adventure.

Perry Silver, Falling Creek Camp, Tuxedo, NC

We would take turns reading the Letters page of *Penthouse Forum* out loud at night. Everyone else would lie in their bunks and jerk off furiously. You would hear the narrator, and the mass creaking of poorly constructed camp beds in the darkness of night.

Nick Kroll, Camp Wildwood, Bridgton, ME

One of the great mysteries of our summer was who took a dump on one of the senior counselors' front porch. This is Adam inspecting the evidence.

Michael Cohen
Camp Louemma, Sussex, NJ
1991

Jacobs Camp, Utica, MS
c. 1981

I am writing you to inform you that Josh has shaved his head. I hope this will not cause any problems.

Thank-you
Robert

Michael Jackson
Thriller

Jacobs Camp
Utica, MS
1983

There's probably a good story behind why I defaced this picture, but I honestly can't remember it. Apologies to all involved. We thought the counselor with "Air Head" written on his chest was an ex–Navy Seal. He once taught us how to creep up behind someone and snap their neck. We were eleven.

David Hertog, Camp Cobbossee, Winthrop, ME
1987

I ended up dating Michael (third boy from left with the pageboy haircut). I had a crush on him as a little girl and took a whole roll of photographs of him playing tetherball one summer.

Margie Katz
Camp Tamakwa,
Algonquin Park, ON,
Canada

1981

1982

66

1983

1985

The flipped-up collar was de rigueur. Perhaps it was the Fonzie influence. The greatest memory I have that parallels these photos is how good music was then. The most important thing I got out of camp was my love and knowledge of music. The Clash's *London Calling,* Bruce Springsteen's *Darkness on the Edge of Town,* Joe Jackson's *Look Sharp,* the Police's *Outlandos d' Amour.* TDK C-90's were our Limewire in those days, except the music was way better.

Jon Cohen, Camp Towanda, Honesdale, PA
Clockwise from above: 1980, 1981, 1983

DEAR SCOTT BLONKIN

BY AJ JACOBS

AJ Jacobs
Camp Powhatan
Otisfield, ME
1981

Dear Scott Blonkin:

I'm sorry. I'm sorry on behalf of every camper in Bunk 12 of Camp Powhatan in 1981. I'm sorry on behalf of myself.

I'm sorry we mocked your tic, the one where you puckered your lips every thirty seconds.

I'm sorry we bet you five Kit Kat bars that you couldn't go a whole day without puckering your lips. I'm sorry we spent the rest of the day puckering our own lips and saying, "Oh, that feels so good. It's soooo good to pucker the lips," until you broke down and puckered your lips and lost the candy.

I'm sorry for spraying Lysol on your arm and lighting it on fire. Actually, I think Matt Rivkin did that. But sorry anyway.

I'm sorry we figured out—and I can't remember how we figured this out—that if we sang "All Around the Mulberry Bush" in a particularly menacing manner, you would burst into tears. The key was to put real aggression into the song. Spit out the syllables like they were a foul-tasting food, especially the "pop goes the weasel" part. I'm sorry we spent the rest of the summer singing that song to you.

I'm sorry we'd go up to you and say, very quickly, "Hi Scott, how you doing, Scott, bye Scott," then walk away, leaving you sputtering in frustration, still formulating your response of "I'm fine."

I'm sorry for the whole weird bathroom incident, of which I can't remember the exact details. I think it went something like this: In the bathroom wall that adjoined your bed, there was a hole the size of a half-dollar, and we put masking tape over the hole, but the masking tape kept disappearing and we assumed you took it off so that you could peer at us while we peed at night, which may or may not have been the case, so we conspired to surround your bed one night after lights-out, all eight of us, and we pulled down our pajamas and underwear down to our knees, and then one of us flicked on the lights and we all screamed so that you woke up and were confronted with the sight of eight prepubescent penises, which we hoped would (a) intimidate you and (b) give you an overdose of what you wanted, so that you'd be cured and leave the masking tape on. You were, in fact, freaked out and screamed for a long time. Sorry about that, too.

I'm sorry we told and retold the story of how you were on second base during a softball game and someone—maybe John Fein—hit a glorious long ball over the left fielder's head and we shouted, "Come home, Blonkin! Come home!" and so you simply followed orders and made a beeline for home plate and ran right over the pitcher's mound.

I'm sorry we pounced on you that time you described your sunburn as "red as a lightbulb," and we pointed out over and over to you that lightbulbs aren't red. I'm sorry we spent the rest of the summer describing everything red, maroon, rust, or burgundy as "red as a lightbulb."

I'm sorry for making fun of you for saying that you were "shaking like a leaf" during your bar mitzvah. We thought you had misspoken, because leaves don't shake. But I realize now that is, in fact, a common idiom. Sorry about that.

I'm sorry we eavesdropped on your conversation with Jimmy the counselor when you said you felt like the "boy in the plastic bubble." I'm sorry we secretly felt ashamed but didn't admit it and congratulated ourselves on a job well done.

I'm sorry boys are such cruel bastards. That I was such a cruel bastard myself. Does it help you to know that I was the one who was getting beaten up during the school year? I was the Scott Blonkin of my school? And that when I found myself on the side of the bullies instead of the bullees, I was so excited I practically popped a boner?

Probably not.

Does it make you feel better to know that I refuse to send my sons to an all-boys camp, because I now know that the level of cruelty at all-boys camps is about equal to Abu Ghraib? Probably not.

Does it help you to know I consider my treatment of you one of the two or three low points in my life as a moral being? And that I've tried, without success, to Google you, hoping to God to discover that you lead a well-adjusted life and are not in prison for firing off a rifle from the top of a tower?

Probably not.

If I see you again, I'll buy you five Kit Kat bars. I promise.

Your friend,

It pelted with rain one day. We all headed back to the bunks to await instructions for whatever rainy day activity was in the works. Cabin fever sets in. We became a little restless and decided that the moment called for a little mischief. A bunch of us changed into our swim trunks, donned our flip-flops, and tore out onto the lower field for some good ol' fashion mud sliding. The field was just perfectly slick that day.

Matthew Rosen, Lake Owego Camp, Greeley, PA
1992

Born to Run

**"Together we could break this trap
We'll run till we drop, baby we'll never go back"
—Bruce Springsteen**

Because you had to do something to kill the daylight hours to make it through to nighttime and—let's face it—only the geeks liked to read, most camps featured a wider array of competitive sporting activity than the Moscow Olympics. Being athletic was a fast track to popularity, and all that year-round coaching Mom and Dad sprung for paid off, as the supremely gifted coasted effortlessly around the tennis clay, softball diamond, or basketball court. Those less physically inclined were left to find their niche amid the sanctuary of the rifle range, Ping-Pong table, or stables.

At camps where sports were the dominant human value for both boys and girls, everyone dreamed of shooting a trophy-clinching, buzzer-beating three-pointer at the intercamp matchups. Some, like the two-day Maine/New Hampshire tourney, were legendary, just like the NCAA finals but a lot more Jewish. Donning custom-made T-shirts or black hoodies, these miniature Larry Byrds hit the court to the sounds of Springsteen's "No Surrender" blaring from tinny speakers behind them.

The era we are celebrating was that of William Perry, Mary Lou Retton, and Andre the Giant, but, more significantly, it was also when Michael Jordan and Nike revolutionized the way we thought about what to wear to play the game—any game. Scan the photos that follow and spot the kids who arrived with a trunk full of specialized sneakers for every sport, and those who wore the same pair of shitty Reebok high-tops all summer.

Jacobs Camp
Utica, MS
1982

73

Josh Weiss
Camp Manitou, Oakland, ME
1986

At school, I was a spazzy kid who was not good at sports. But at camp—I was so good at everything I tried. Softball. Volleyball. I was the captain. It was a confidence game. At school, playing dodgeball, my strategy was to let myself get hit as quickly as possible. But at camp, I found moves. The ball was a weapon. I heard people shout, "Watch out for Weiner." They feared me.

Jenny Weiner, Camp Emerson, Hinsdale, MA

We would put on the baggiest, most ghetto sportswear we could find. And then when other camps started to do the same, we would run out in our pajamas and robes. What a statement we made: I can just roll out of bed in my robe and destroy you.

Ross Martin, Camp Harlam, Kresgeville, PA

Floor hockey is a major part of Jewish camp. It's not a factor anywhere else in the real world outside of the Special Olympics. Floor hockey is less dangerous and more cerebral ice hockey. Most important, parents don't complain about their kids playing it. Seneca dominated every camp at every age. We would play Sigue Sigue Sputnik's "Shoot It Up" during warmups to put the fear of God in our opponents.

Mark Miller, Camp Seneca Lake, Honesdale, PA

Wekeela Illustrated

SPORTS
CHAMPIONSHIPS
COVER PHOTO
CAMPER
OF THE YEAR
1986 SEASON
IT'S SO FUN

I was nothing close to camper of the year. I was just a nerdy girl with a paralyzing crush on one of the guys on the tennis staff. This photo shoot was the closest I ever got to the sports field.

Sharon Brous
Camp Wekeela
Canton, ME
1986

JASON STRAUSS: IS IT THE SHOES?

When the Summer Camp
Hall of Fame is one day built, we pray that the Veteran's Committee views Camp Winadu's Jason Strauss as a shoo-in. More explosive than the Boz, faster than Matt Biondi, and with more flair than Vitas Gerulaitis, he mastered a dizzying number of disciplines, making two-sports star Bo Jackson look uncoordinated.

Jason Strauss
Camp Winadu
Springfield, MA
1985–88

I can recall feeling very cool because I was a terrible athlete—except when it came
to gymnastics. It was the only sport that I was better at than everyone else.

Shana Madoff, Camp Scatico, Elizaville, NY
1980

Lindsay Weiss
Camp Matoaka, Smithfield, ME
1987

Jacobs Camp
Utica, MS
1980

DEAR HUNTER

BY TODD ROSENBERG

Some kids were good at soccer. I was the kid who would kick the ball wide when I had an open net. Some kids were good at swimming. To get a "blue chip" you had to float for five minutes in the lake. I could never float. My legs would always sink, and still do to this day. Sure, I took pride in the cheeseboard I crafted in woodshop or the occasional win at the game "Pig" in the cafeteria. (Pig: Everyone at the dinner table has to quietly put one finger on the side of their nose. The last person to notice the game is being played is too involved with their food, hence Pig.) But my calling—my talent—my world—was archery.

I loved archery from the beginning. Maybe it was the sense of control. The solitary nature of the sport. The stillness of it. The challenge was mental. It was all about balance and breathing. Most sports are a team effort in one way or another but archery is all about you. The victory is 100 percent yours. Any mistake leaves only one person to blame. As a natural loner of sorts, I think I appreciated this public isolation. It was my comfort zone.

Plus, I was great at it! For me a bad shot wouldn't be in the dirt or over the net and onto the soccer field. For me a bad shot would be in the blue ring. Or on a very bad day in the shameful black or white. But that was very rare, as I was the best archer in camp.

Not everyone agreed, however. One person would beg to differ. That person was Miles Mintz. Miles was my age. Slightly shorter than me, with the standard '70s bowl cut. We never spoke much but somehow we often found each other side by side. Toeing the line and shooting, shot for shot. We were way beyond using the plastic crap stick bows provided by the camp. Those days were long since past. We both had our own straight bows. I shot with a Ben Pearson brand bow while Miles went with the Bear brand. Of course, either he bought a Bear because I had a Ben Pearson or vice versa. We certainly didn't want to "follow" each other in any way.

Every year at camp there was Camp Olympics. It was sort of like Color War stuff but with eight teams. I, of course, was the chosen "archer" for the team I was on. There was no discussion or debate. I was so superior, so much better than everyone else, that sometimes I felt guilt about my skill. As if God himself pointed at me and said, "You will be an archer!" Like I was one of those Greek gods maybe with a bow. Whatshisface? Hermes? No, the other guy. Whatshisface's brother or something.

Sure, there were other contests over the course of the summer. And yes, I admit I'd lost now and then to Miles Mintz (maybe on a particularly gnatty day or something). Sure, I was capable of losing. And whenever that fluke happened, I'd always note the smirk on Miles's face. That smiley assumption that somehow I'd lost my touch. I'd take note. I'd vow revenge.

My very last summer at camp, I got a Ben Pearson compound bow (those hunter-looking bows with the pulley system) in the off-season. I had moved far beyond what other campers were doing. If they were shooting at thirty yards, I'd be off to the side shooting at seventy yards. My new bow was awesome to other campers. At my camp, most kids didn't necessarily go home to shoot elk, so cool weapons weren't common.

Todd Rosenberg
Camp Mah-Kee-Nac
Lenox, MA
1979

All summer long I shot with my compound bow. I couldn't even use it at the closer targets because the arrows would blast straight through and out the other side (*cough*–awesome!). Sometimes I'd take a break from shooting at the actual targets to shoot at the wooden stand that held the target. At some point Miles might have seen me "miss the target" and hit the wood. He may have even snorted a laugh. I wouldn't even bother to let him know that it wasn't a miss–that I was actually aiming for that knot in the wood. He would, of course, never believe it.

Anyway, toward the end of the summer with Camp Olympics approaching in a couple weeks, I asked Dave, the head archery counselor, if I could use my compound bow in Olympics. After all, at this point Miles had an expensive and impressive Bear straight bow. Dave said I could. Granted, allowing me to use a compound bow wasn't a fair decision. A compound bow had the advantage of holding the string back longer and easier without giving up any power, allowing a smoother release.

I realized this was an unfair advantage of sorts, but if Dave said it was OK for me to use the compound bow I felt no need to argue. Miles would just have to take an extra-good beating this year.

The day of the Olympics finally arrived. Miles and I were set to compete head-to-head along with other scrubby archers from other teams. The game was elimination. Eight rounds. Lowest score walks. One by one. Until it was down to two. Everyone knew that those two would be Miles and me.

I took my compound bow out of its case and walked over toward the targets, looking at the other campers like an Archery God. With a bow that was given to me by Hermes himself! (No, wait! It was Apollo! Hermes ran fast or something?) A crowd had formed to watch the event. To cheer on their teams.

My crowd and Miles's were about the same size. As I stepped to the line I wore a quiver on my back with pristine "real feather" arrows. Miles opened his yap.

Miles complained that it was unfair for me to use my compound bow, that the advantage of the compound bow was too unfair. Miles had known for a couple weeks that he was going up against my compound bow, but he sneakily saved his protest for the day of the Olympics. And to my horror, Counselor Dave caved. He admitted he was wrong to allow the compound bow in the first place, and said I had to revert to my old bow.

I headed to the archery shed and dusted off my old straight bow. I felt my heart sink; I hadn't used it all summer. It's a completely different process to shoot with a straight bow. It's a slightly different vibe. Straight bows are about stillness and breathing, while compound bows are more about the release and timing. I restrung it and walked to the line. Miles had a big smirk on his face as if he'd already won. I admit I was nervous about it. I felt completely out of practice.

Miles shot first. He had a nice grouping. Out of the six shots he probably hit three yellows and three reds. My first shot, I stepped up to the line, took an arrow from my quiver, clipped it to the string, and pulled back. I held my shot for a while and tried to get my breathing under control. I wasn't used to holding back that much pressure. I didn't take the shot. I relaxed the bow and took a deep breath. Miles must have had an archery boner. Seeing my first sign of weakness was surely exciting for him.

I pulled the string back a second time and held it. I felt the old juices start flowing as things got very still. The outside world blurred away until it was just me and the target. Me. And old yellow. The gold. I released the first shot and it hit dead center bull's-eye. I knew it was going to be dead center before I even released the string.

84

Miles must have known things were not going according to plan, but may have written that shot off as lucky. My second shot cleared away all doubt. Zeus must have been smiling down on his Apollo that day, because I was now in the zone, was fueled by my anger at Miles for trying to throw me off my game. And I certainly wiped the smile off his face, along with all doubt as to who was the Archer King, when my second shot not only hit dead center but splintered the first arrow in an explosion of feathers.

Archery occupied second-tier status at Greylock, which actually made it more fun and relaxing for me. The sweaty palms came during the high-pressure, big-money sports of basketball, soccer, and baseball that we would play during "intercamps" against Winadu and Mah-kee-nac. Don't be deceived by the Mickey Mouse shirt. I'll hunt your ass down.

Jon Jacoby
Camp Greylock, Becket, MA
1988

Andrew Jacobs
Camp Takajo,
Naples, ME
1984

This picture looks like a Hezbollah propaganda shot. I liked riflery, but I don't remember being that good at it. The younger campers got BB guns, like the one I'm holding, and the older kids got real .22s.

David Hertog
Camp Androscoggin, Wayne, ME
1983

Camp Mah-Kee-Nac
Lenox, MA
c. 1984

Perry Silver
Falling Creek Camp
Tuxedo, NC
1987

These guys were imported from Pakistan to act as our tennis coaches and live out the American dream.

Sharna Goldseker
Camp Bryn Mawr, Honesdale, PA
1989

Our camp had a Jamaican tennis pro slumming by teaching privileged white kids how to hit a ball. He kept it interesting for himself by fucking with us. He liked to force me into the shower fully dressed—and we are talking my favorite Andre Agassi Day-Glo shirt with the Roy Lichtenstein print, and John McEnroe Nike sneakers, the first cross-trainers with the fluorescent green bubble. If you weren't wearing the right sneakers you could be destroyed. He ordered me to belt out a version of Whitney Houston's "The Greatest Love of All" in front of the other kids in the bunk. I remember getting to the line about "you can't take away my dignity," looking at him straight in the eye with water cascading down my face and just feeling overwhelmed by the irony of it all.

Mark Ronson, Camp Amherst, Amherst, MA

Me showing off by playing tennis and letting my parents see my awesome "ready stance," despite the fact that I had broken my arm that summer.

Caren Cohen, Point O'Pines, Brant Lake, NY
1977

Tom Rosenberg
Camp Scatico, Elizaville, NY
1977

THE INVENTED SPORTS OF CAMP

When and why were these sports removed from the Olympics? The following games were played competitively at camps across the country, becoming the subject of serious strategic conversations about how to develop the competitive edge that would deliver victory. Campers could stay up all night engrossed in animated conversation about Human Croquet, which fired the imagination in a way that tennis or baseball never could.

Lightning Ball
Softball with tennis racket and ball. Though everyone really just wanted to play tennis.

Adam Espstein, Camp Akiba, Reeders, PA

Human Croquet
Extremely competitive. Counselors were the wickets. Teams would dive through their legs. Even the fat ones, which could be like a road crash.

Rachel Kane, Camp Che-Na-Wah, Minerva, NY

Midnight Bombardment
You would wake up the bunk below in the middle of the night and make them go out onto the volleyball court with the lights on. The thirteen-year-olds and counselors would take on the fourteen- and fifteen-year olds. The counselors would wipe the kids out. This was never played anywhere near visiting day due to heavy bruising.

Anonymous, Camp Cedar, Casco, ME

Dodgeball with Frisbee and Ball
A brutal version that was guaranteed to get nasty. The secret was to avoid the Frisbee.

Ken Freimann, Camp Norwich, Huntington, MA

Prisoner Ball
Dodgeball with a net. Its popularity was due to its being located by the biggest trees, for maximum shade, and right between girls' and boys' camp. We would vie to get a double volleyball block, which would soon disintegrate into twenty-five kids lying around in a line massaging each other with the volleyball laying there idly on the court. I was under those trees when I found out Elvis died.

Michael Wolfson, Camp Boiberik, Rhinebeck, NY

Squeamish
This game was like a cross between handball and soccer or lacrosse. It was played on a field with lacrosse goals upside-down. Another one of the rules—the players had to be barefoot and wear only boxers. This game was quickly banned by the camp staff for inciting violence. So we created a variation where you played in shorts instead of boxers and called it Jamaican Ball.

Andrew Goldberg, Camp Wildwood, Bridgton, ME

We used to play a game called Tennis Baseball, where a tennis racquet (yes, that's a Prince) and a tennis ball were used instead of baseballs, though we did use gloves and mitts. I was not a good tennis player, but I had sloppy joyous fun playing this game. Note my scraped knee.

Adam Epstein, Camp Akiba, Reeders, PA
1983

Brad Grossman
Camp Weequanic
Lakewood, PA
1988

FIVE SONGS TO PLAY DURING BASKETBALL SHOOTAROUND

As any pro athlete will attest, basketball games are most often won or lost during the shoot-around, when the team who looks more coordinated and confident can take control of the mental game. And so the music selected to blare out of—albeit it tinny—speakers was often the critical element that could keep a team loose during layups and inspire them to go on to drink from the cup of victory. Among the most popular, in no particular order, were:

- Big Country, "In a Big Country"
- Earth Wind and Fire, "Got to Get You into My Life"
- Jackson Five, "ABC"
- New Edition, "Candy Girl" (basically the same song as "ABC")
- Phil Collins, "I Missed Again"

Tom Rosenberg
Camp Scatico, Elizaville, NY
1977

Kevin Harrison
Camp Sequoia
Rock Hill, NY
1984

I believe that everyone exists on a bell curve. Jewish camp is far down that bell curve. In the same way that a nerd at camp can pass himself off as a player with the ladies, so an average baller by real-life standards can pass at Ramah as a sports god. We were crazy about basketball. Tisha B'Av is a big Jewish fast day and the day for the annual basketball game between the fasters and the nonfasters, which bizarrely the fasters always won. I would lay money on the fact that one kid, Avi, was the greatest living fasting basketball player ever. The rest of the year he was shit. But on an empty stomach he was unstoppable.

David Light
Camp Ramah in the Poconos, Lake Como, PA

Camp Kennybrook, Monticello, NY
c. 1983

When I was ten or eleven, I was a wrestling fan. I brought a stack of wrestling magazines to camp. Later on, we would sit around and dream up fake names and personalities for ourselves. My partner was Ben Krull, who was obsessed with basketball. At nighttime, while the rest of us were up to no good, he would perform dribbling drills on the basketball court using chairs as opponents in the dark. He became Gentleman Ben Krull, who was modeled after Bruno Sammartino and Bob Backlund—a milk-drinking, gimmick-free good guy. I was Rodeo Doug Herzog, modeled after Black Jack Mulligan—jeans, cowboy boots/hat, lasso, and a glove. My signature move involved my lasso and my gloved hand. Things moved fast from there and we soon had the idea of actually putting on a wrestling match. We pulled out the gym mats and went for it. Rodeo Doug Herzog and Gentleman Ben Krull were of course the undisputed Tag Team Champions! But hey, we started the whole thing . . . and we were the biggest wrestling fans.

Doug Herzog, Camp Scatico, Elizaville, NY
1978

Tom Rosenberg
Camp Scatico
Elizaville, NY
1977

94

NFL football pro Herschel Walker visited our camp. He threw a ball to every single camper. It was amazing how long it took.

Scott Rothschild
Camp Kennybrook
Monticello, NY
1988

I was a very physical basketball player, to compensate for my lack of speed. At camp, fouls were rarely called, and pushing was tacitly allowed. I was all about the rebound. Inside camp there was a fierce intercampus competition. We practiced for hours and hours. The team two years younger than us was just plain dominant. Our team was especially poor. We were just awful. Then in my junior year, a big kid from Argentina, Itai, joined us out of nowhere. He was a giant—six foot four—with soft hands and a great hook shot. When he came he was the gentlest, nicest guy the whole summer. The next year, he came back, and I still don't know what had happened in between, but he was a huge dick. He was abusive, petulant, aggressive, he had fights . . . and he took us over the top . . . out of nowhere. We were the champions.

Mik Moore, Camp Tel Yehudah, Barryville, NY

Play Day was when six camps would compete mano a mano—each hosting a different sport. The great anticipation was less about the competition, as we traditionally kicked ass, than about seeing the other camps. The hosts—girls no different from us—would tour us around and we would see their setups, their bunks stuffed with boxes of Guess jeans and Conair hair dryers, their walls spray-painted pink, their manicured playing fields, their dining room setups . . . like country clubs. And we would all return at night and share our stories about these girls who were nasty, materialistic, and worst of all, shit at sports. And it felt like affirmation of our camp and our traditions. The reality was, these girls were very much the same as us—from the same homes, and the same high schools.

Vanessa Kroll, Camp Walden, Denmark, ME

I fell in love twice my first year at camp. Once with Jody Weinberg and once with the concept of horseback riding, which I had always romanticized because of the Clint Eastwood spaghetti westerns I used to watch with my dad and brothers. My second camp experience was not as positive. I began my summer by running after the car of my leaving parents and grandmother, crying my eyes out in front of my soon-to-be cabin mates. Predictably, they were not very nice to me after that, and I found my one friend in Kimba, a tall, dark brown, beautiful horse that was known to be tough to deal with. Every time I picked and cleaned Kimba's hooves, he would buck slightly and attempt to break free. I learned to position myself away from the buck, creating a "safety zone." The horse trainer saw Kimba buck at me one afternoon and came over to "show me how to properly clean a horse's hoof." Kimba bucked as usual, but this time found his mark, breaking three of the trainer's ribs. I pleaded and pleaded and, for some strange reason, was granted the right to keep taking care of Kimba and to not have the horse sent to the glue factory, which would have deprived me of my one and only true friend. Kimba still appears in my dreams every few years.

David Katznelson
Skylake Yosemite Camp, Wishen, CA
1980

Arts & Crafts

paint -n- brush

"macrame"

with

slip casting

jewelry

potter's wheel ~

Lisa, Onie, Teri & Barb

Hip to be Square

"Don't tell me that I'm crazy
Don't tell me I'm nowhere"
—Huey Lewis and the News

How could those who are too fat, lazy, or stoned to take to the sports field be occupied for an entire summer? The answer lay in the Arts and Crafts room, where campers could huddle together and fritter away their time like prisoners in a minimum security facility. Those most likely to go postal were confined to the photographic darkroom. The rest experimented with pottery, macramé, and charcoal if they had a modicum of talent, or tie-dyeing if they did not. Tracy Chapman's debut album was faintly audible the entire summer of 1988 in the Arts and Crafts room. Every camp had one kid who, in an act straight out of *Rain Man,* spent the summer hunkered down in the corner, only to unveil a scale model of the Leaning Tower of Pisa made out of matchsticks on the last day of camp.

Camp Matoaka
Smithfield, ME
1984

99

I started camp at age ten. This was a time when music had just started to overwhelm my life. I was playing piano and drums. I was sent off to this sports camp and I fell head over heels with Arts and Crafts. I loved the smell of wood. I loved heavy machinery. I spent all of my free time in the woodshed. I had always been fascinated by pictures of Hendrix in music magazines, so I decided to make a guitar just like his . . . a lefty playing a right-handed guitar.

It took me all summer to craft this air guitar. Cutting. Etching the frets. Sanding the body. Painting with coat after coat of enamel. Walter the woodwork guy was like a father figure to me. He was overweight. In his sixties. The kindest, most humble man imaginable. A master of the band saw. And probably one of the loneliest men in the world as a woodwork instructor in an all-boys sports camp. He taught me to appreciate craftsmanship, with his Zen quality. He would appear over my shoulder and whisper, "Good work."

Scott Jacoby, Camp Greylock, Becket, MA
1982

Silk-screening was my favorite. When I was really homesick, I could go to Arts and Crafts and sob and still accomplish something. Older kids made Sex Pistols designs but I had my dog missing me at home. The shirt was a tribute. Every time I wore it at camp, it was like he was there. This was of my English bull terrier, Butch. I made them for my whole family as a symbol of how much I wanted to come home.

Katie Weinberg, French Woods, Hancock, NY
1988

**THE STAGE**

Center Stage

"A joker's dance before the king
Jangling beads, a silver ring"
—Indigo Girls

There is Broadway, there is Off Broadway, and there is Off Off Broadway. Take the last category to the power of fifty and you come close to capturing the theatrical stylings of camp. The camp theater department was a world with a surplus of good intention and a deficit of talent. The directors, a mix of young gay male wannabes with big dreams and middle-aged alcoholic has-beens on the way down, oversaw a talent pool that changed little year to year. One or two precocious young things were talented enough to have Hollywood aspirations, with Foxwoods as their plan B. The rest of the cast consisted of popular jocks who had been forced to participate in an effort to encourage others to take theater seriously, and assorted malingerers who padded around the back of the stage blowing their cues until the curtain came down. Whether the performance was of a well-worn classic such as *Oliver!, The Pirates of Penzance,* or *Guys and Dolls,* often produced without a script, or a more avant-garde mashup involving the characters of *Scooby-Doo* and the music of Pink Floyd, all were given a good butchering onstage, with the same costumes from the previous production, repurposed within an inch of their lives.

The lip syncs and skits were another animal altogether, and stood as the perfect way to glimpse the creativity and innovation that have made this country great. Sketches from *Saturday Night Live* or videos that had been scored into campers' collective subconscious via heavy rotation on MTV, from the Go-Go's to the Fat Boys, were translated to the confines of the camp stage, and often improved as a result.

This is "Rock Around the Ages." Each bunk was assigned a decade to perform. We look very reggae but this is meant to be Milli Vanilli.

Aaron Bisman and
Jacob Harris
Camp Ramah, Ojai, CA
1992

This was part of a bunk lip-synching contest, the best part of the summer. We totally *won* with this rendition of "'Cause I'm a Blonde" by Julie Brown, in these wigs we made ourselves out of brown paper bags and yellow string. They were funny-looking, but being the actress that I am, when I put mine on, I totally felt blond.

Ariel Silberman, Camp Echo Lark, Poyntelle, PA
1986

"Puttin' on the Hits" (we got this idea from the TV show of the same name), a precursor to karaoke. Each group had to sing and dance to a song of their choice. Four of us did a rap song called "Basketball" by Kurtis Blow.

Adam Wallach, Camp Ramah in the Berkshires, Wingdale, NY
1985

Ken Freimann
Camp Norwich
Huntington, MA
1984

We came up with this high-concept piece we called the "Nutcracker Suite," which involved us holding up these seat cushions and hitting each other in the nuts with them, and at the end of the act the cushions spelled out the word *P.A.I.N.*

Will Abers, Camp Brotherhood/Sisterhood, San Bernardino, CA
1986

I honestly do not remember winning any talent shows, despite this move.

Lauren Goldstein, KenWood Camp, Kent, CT
1990

Every camp had an outcast who was so weird they became a superstar. Ours was Seth. He had a facial deformity and such bizarre habits. He learned to play a mean guitar and would play "Mellow Yellow" all summer. When it stormed he would put on a hood and run outside even though the trees were swaying and scream, "LSD! LSD! LSD!" In real life such a character would be avoided, but at camp these characters became cult icons, heroes who would get parts specially written for them in camp plays.

Simmy Kunstawitz, Camp Ramah in the Berkshires, Wingdale, NY

I was big boned, but I was a very good mover and dancer, or at least I thought so until our choreographer once exclaimed out loud, "Look at that girl in the front, she looks like she's got a dick." She then went on to give us a lecture about how some of us had gotten to the stage that "when we wear spandex we should be thinking about what we wear under that leotard," staring me right in the eye. I did not know what to make of this—mine were not real boobs, they were more rolls of fat.

Sara Barron, Summer Stage, Highland Park, IL

Talent Night. The song
was "Our Lips Are
Sealed." Classic Go-Go's.

Julie Jacobs
Camp Lochearn
Post Mills, VT
1983

"Vacation,"
by the Go-Go's.

Karen Lauterstein
KenWood Camp
Kent, CT
1986

LIP-SYNC

BY EVAN TURNER

The lip-sync contest was absolutely the biggest thing at our camp. Not Color War. Not Visiting Day. It was "Puttin' on the Hits." To win was the highest accolade—the crown jewel of camp. That, and you got a pizza party.

I would spend ten months of the year poring over cassette tapes or glued to FM radio hoping to find that perfect song. Something dramatic, something catchy, something that told an epic story. My first year of camp, the bar was set impossibly high, as the oldest bunk did a tear-jerking rendition of Harry Chapin's classic "Cat's in the Cradle." Sure, we were just ten-year-olds, but somehow we understood the song's heart-wrenching message of balancing work and family.

Years passed and we watched as classics like "Bohemian Rhapsody" and "Paradise by the Dashboard Light" were snapped up. And I wasn't going to be burned again, like the time we chose Weird Al's "The Brady Bunch"—a fluff piece that went for laughs and got none. And, of course, there was the infamous debacle when we chose Chicago's "Stay the Night" and tanked. It had no story at all. Who wants to watch a bunch of prepubescent boys strum their tennis rackets like guitars for five minutes? Not our panel of counselor judges, that's for sure.

I spent the whole next school year determined to find my own magical song. Finally, it came to me. Billy Joel's triumphant "Goodnight Saigon," the tale of a man coping with post-traumatic stress disorder from his days in the jungles of Vietnam. It was freaking perfect.

When I unpacked my trunk that summer, I also unpacked my dream. I was thirteen and wasn't getting any younger. If I was going to win that pizza party, this year was it. I played the lead role, a war-torn soldier reminiscing about his days fighting Charlie. I put baby powder in my hair, giving it the effect of looking gray. This was high production value. My bunk mates would enact a bloody Vietnam War flashback. Half of the bunk wore flip-flops, connoting they were Vietcong. The other half wore college T-shirts, to show they were American soldiers. Our performance—set to a cheap strobe light—was masterful, leading up to the explosive climax where we all embraced (except the dead Vietcong lying on the stage), as Joel's lyrics hit their crescendo, proclaiming, "And we will all go down together. Yes we will all go down together!" Victory was in the bag.

But we didn't count on a Queen medley wiping us out. What a gimmick. "Fat Bottomed Girls" dissolving into "Bicycle Race" into "Radio Ga Ga" into a toe-tapping finale of the Flash Gordon theme. Sure, it was cute, but where was the drama? The heartfelt lyrics? The strobe light? The pizza party was theirs.

I cried on our walk back to the bunk. Hard. I had let everyone down. But vengeance would be mine. I had one year left and this Jew wasn't going down without a fight.

The next summer, I ended up in the fattest bunk in camp. Everyone attributed it to the fact that Gameboy had come out and all we wanted to do was sit around and play Tertris instead of more athletic pursuits like floor hockey. I decided to use our weakness as our strength. We were going to lip-synch to the rap hit "The Fat Boys Are Back!" Sure, it wasn't Oscar material, but it was gonna be a box office hit. Something the people could rally behind.

We took the stage with pillows crammed into our Champion T-shirts and sweatpants. We showered the audience with candy bars—a calculated move to buy votes. We rapped and did the worm like never before. Our biggest competition was one of the most blatantly exploitative moves in camp history, a performance of "God Bless the U.S.A.," complete with flag waving and saluting. Even I got a little misty, as much as I tried to hate it. But the panel of counselors who voted did not have to deliberate long. We were victorious and drunk with joy. It was the greatest moment of my life, jumping onstage and hugging each other with pillows spilling out of our shirts. In my little world—for just that moment—I was a camp legend. Eat that, Freddie Mercury.

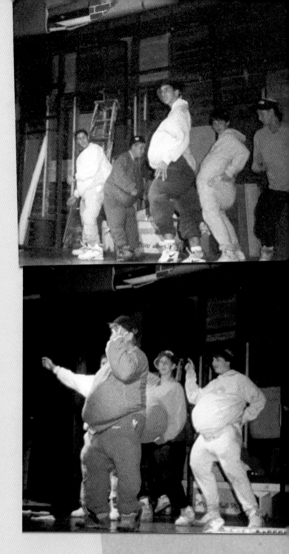

Evan Turner
Camp Echo Lark
Poyntelle, PA
1987

We were fourteen and we decided to do a musical version of Elie Wiesel's *Dawn*. The book is about the Holocaust and the creation of the State of Israel. Heavy stuff. We adapted the book ourselves and had the idea of setting it to the music of Billy Joel. Unfortunately it rained heavily during our performance and water started to leak, then pour, through the roof. The grand finale of our performance was the entire cast singing "Goodnight Saigon," the Joel song that opens with the sound of whirling helicopter blades. By then, rain was seeping through the scenery. We were singing away on stage in our Holocaust outfits laughing, aware we had just turned this most somber of books into a comedy.

Rachel Cohen, Camp Tel Yehudah, Barryville, NY

Joseph and the Amazing Technicolor Dreamcoat was the big one. I had used my bar mitzvah money to buy a Yamaha CS 15—the first non-Moog synthesizer. I brought it to camp and the director encouraged my using it. I got to play the synth at the show.

Jon Steingart, Camp Hess Kramer, Malibu, CA

Camp Ramah, Grenada Hills, CA
date unknown

It's the annual Mr. & Mrs. Mobjack competition at the now-defunct Mobjack Sailing Camp in southern Virginia. Each cabin would enter a camper, both boys and girls, dressed in drag to compete. Those are the two counselors who were hosting the pageant (in the dining hall), with me in the flag towel. I ended up losing to a younger camper who had water balloons for boobs. Notice the friendship bracelets and the spoon bracelet (right) made from a stolen cafeteria spoon.

Matt Spitz, Mobjack Sailing Camp, Mobjack Bay, VA
1991

Jenna Fallon
Camp Edward Isaacs
Holmes, NY
1989

Redemption Song

> "Won't you help to sing
> These songs of freedom"
> —Bob Marley

Whoever brungeth the bunk's boom box, or at least, the Sony pastel twin cassette tape recorder, wieldeth the power to dictate the soundtrack that drove the summer. The tapes you brought to camp defined you. Were you a Hall & Oates, Queen, Run-DMC, or Howard Jones kind of person? The answer to that question would inevitably change over the course of a summer, because there were few finer places than camp to be turned on to new sounds. African-American counselors would rock your world with a little Earth, Wind, and Fire; soccer coaches from England introduced you to Manchester's finest, the Stone Roses; or charismatic female bunk heads would flip on the Indigo Girls debut and blow the collective mind of the entire girls' side.

These songs were not just listened to, they were memorized. Approximately 80 percent of the summer in camp was spent singing. Many bunk mates spent rest hour rewinding Andrew Dice Clay or Rob Base and DJ EZ Rock tapes over and over so they could learn the lyrics and blurt them out a cappella in the dining room to assert bunk identity. These artists and more would find their way onto the mix tape everyone left camp with at the end of the summer. In an eclectic cascade of sound, that one song that felt like it was played repetitively in every bunk and at every social—be it by The J. Geils Band, R.E.M., or Suzanne Vega—could happily coexist with that Led Zeppelin, The Who, or Phish song you spent the summer listening to lying out on the baseball field late at night, looking at the stars, imagining what drugs might feel like.

Camp Henry James
Utica, MS
ca. 1980

DE LA SOUL, KOOL MOE DEE, SLICK RICK, SPECIAL ED
TOO SHORT, KWAME, NWA, L.L. COOL J, PUBLIC ENEMY
BIG DADDY KANE, YOUNG M.C., MARLEY MARL
K9 POSSE, CHUCK CHILLOUT, KOOL CHIP

maxell

A side
...off, A Little Bit of Soap, De La
...Desciption, I Can Do Anything - De La Soul
...Work - Kool Moe Dee
...ren's Story - Slick Rick
...t Trippin - Too Short
...ng - Special Ed
...2 Get Down - Kwamé
...ght Outta Compton - NWA
...e Type of Guy - L.L. Cool J
...is Military - K9 Posse

B side
Club Scene - Special Ed
Me, Myself, And I - De La Soul
Fight The Power - Public Enemy
Droppin' Em - L.L. Cool J
Lean on Me - Big Daddy Kane
Bust The Move - Young M.C.
The Symphony - Marley Marl
Hoedown - Special Ed
Ain't Nothin' To It - K9 Posse
Rhythm is The Master - Chuck Chillout

maxell XLII 90

KWAME, DE LA SOUL, EAZY-E, AUDIO TWO, 7A3
SLICK RICK, M.C. HAMMER, PUBLIC ENEMY
KOOL G RAP + D.J. POLO, BIG DADDY KANE, SPECIAL ED

A side
...w We All Know And Love - Kwamé
...fa Taught Me - De La Soul
...y - Dvz-It - Eazy-E
...ont Care - Audio Two
...dian Girl - Slick Rick
...ms of Steel - 7A3
...it Up - M.C. Hammer
...rity of the First World - P.E.
...les In My Lawn - De La Soul
...I To The Riches - Kool G Rap, D.J. Polo

B side
Self Destruction - Stop The Vi...
We Want Eazy - Eaz...
Tread Water - De La...
Mona Lisa - Slick...
Wrath of Kane - Big Dad...
Life is... Too Short - Too S...
I Got it Made - Special...
NWA - Gangsta Gan...
They Want Money - Kool M...

Camp was part of my musical evolution. When I started at twelve, rap music was for black people, was feared by white parents, and barely on the radar of white kids. By the time I left at age seventeen, it was 1991 and rap was faintly audible everywhere. In the late 1980s everyone was listening to Def Leppard. "Pour Some Sugar on Me" was the sound of every camp social. A small handful of us came to camp with a love of this new rap sound. It is one of the great, untold stories: the role Jewish summer camp played in the spread of rap music to the suburbs of America. It brought kids together from all corners of the country to swap local sounds. I came from New York with my Public Enemy, EMD, Heavy D, and Gang Starr tapes. A girl named Arielle came from Seattle with her love of Seattle hip-hop, which meant Sir Mix-a-Lot. Dave came from Chicago and brought his house sound. Next thing you know, campers were lip-synching to "Paul Revere" at talent night.

Mik Moore, Camp Tel Yehuda, Barryville, NY
1989

Everyone had a pastel-colored Sony boom box that really felt like it made Debbie Gibson sound extra special. In the rest hour, we would all play our bat mitzvah tapes that our rabbis had sent us up to camp with to practice. It was known as the Ralph Lifschitz hour.

Deb Bander, Camp Matoaka, Oakland, ME

Our camp was ruled by song. Impromptu skits could break out at any time, especially during meals. Someone would just stand there doing a surreal mime of playing instruments. It was like YouTube before it happened.

Michael Wolfson, Camp Boiberik, Rhinebeck, NY

I wasn't an extrovert, so standing on tables singing did not come naturally to me. "Oh bagels. Oh bagels. Bagels in the east. Bagels in the west. Machon Bunk is the best." Eighty percent of time in camp was spent singing. The remaining 20 percent was spent Israeli dancing. We danced in the biggest dust bowl. There was no grass. After five minutes kids were keeling over, retching. Day after day we would go back to this place, even though after five minutes your glasses would be covered with dust.

Mik Moore, Camp Tel Yehudah, Barryville, NY

At ten years old I heard the Who for the first time ever on the bus ride home from camp. The guy in front of me had one of those thin double cassette recorders and kept playing "Baba O'Riley" over and over and air piano-ing along. I had been obsessed with music since I was four or five. Sean Cassidy at first. Then I owned every Kiss record. Even *Dynasty*. This was the same year the Who did their original farewell tour. Cable was yet to be invented, so it was broadcast on network TV. December 17, 1982, at Maple Leaf Gardens in Toronto. My sister recorded it on Betamax tape, which cut off during the encore. My whole life from then till I was seventeen was dominated by the Who.

Jordan Kurland, Camp North Star, Hayward, WI

When I was a counselor, I persuaded the camp director to let me teach the kids music. My qualifications were scant. I could play the acoustic guitar badly. I got forty minutes with each group of kids. The only trouble was that I knew no kids' songs. So I went with what I knew and adapted them into camp-friendly tunes. I turned Bad Company's "I Feel Like Making Love" into "I Feel Like Making Lunch."

Mark Ronson, Camp Amherst, Amherst, MA

Josh Weiss
Camp Manitou
Oakland, ME
1987

By the way I can have my walkman — please send that and the D.f Lepord tape as soon and as safe as possible. We can have candy on Visiting Day mom I already go a letter from you. I think I'm going to send a

THE ROCKIN' KNIGHTS OF SUMMER

BY DAVID WAIN

Summer camp was the first place I felt omnipotent. My first summer was 1980, but I didn't truly "arrive" until the summer of '84 when I got off the bus equipped with a new nose. The confidence this gave me felt like I had gotten a power pac in a video game—there was no such thing as a wrong move. My newfound sense of self melded well with the culture of our camp, which was founded on the belief that you did not actually have to do anything at all the whole summer. I spent mornings hanging out in the bunk talking about girls and afternoons relaxing some more, hanging out by the lake. I was left alone, free to think and act on impulse. And that impulse was most often to make out with girls. Music was inextricably intertwined with all of this magic. Camp left me with a deep appreciation for folk songs of the 1960s like "Circle Game" and "Where Have All the Flowers Gone?" But in our bunk—the place where the serious male bonding went down—rock 'n' roll reigned supreme. We had three tapes we would sit around and listen to, in order, all the way through, over and over again:

> *Glass Houses* by Billy Joel
> *Emotional Rescue* by the Rolling Stones
> *Love Stinks* by the J. Geils Band

This was powerful stuff. So, come the summer of 1989, at age nineteen, when I had been out of camp for two years, I felt "the calling." I just had to go back and experience the campfires, open spaces, and sweaty, hot, sexy fun that is camp life one more time. I knew that my key to the door back in

118

was music. I had played drums in several bands in Shaker Heights: Batman and Robin, which specialized in covers of alternative bands like the Pretenders, Dream Syndicate, and Teardrop Explodes; Seven Chinese Brothers, an R.E.M. cover band; and, of course, our tribute to the Smiths, This Charming Band.

I decided to combine my two favorite things and meld the best players from all of my bands into a "supergroup" to play the summer-camp circuit. And the name of that band would be appropriately cheesy and camp-director friendly, The Rockin' Knights of Summer. The band's lineup was:

Scott Harbert—lead guitar/lead vocals
Steve Kelly—bass (and comanager with me)
Dan Kamionkowski—keyboards and rhythm
guitar (and vocals)
Me—drums (and sometimes piano and
sometimes horrible singing)

My father lent us the money to buy a van—a Chevy Model 20. I had a Mac SE-30 and used it to dummy up official-looking letterhead. I sent promotional material to every camp director in Maine and New Hampshire. According to my letter, we, the Rockin' Knights of Summer, were big in Shaker Heights, and because we are all camp alumni, we want to come play a gig at your camp that will blow your campers' minds, and then do a workshop the next day where we teach the kids rock 'n' roll. In return, we asked for $300, dinner and breakfast, and a place to sleep. We should have been more specific on this. We imagined being back in a bunk. The place the directors gave us was most often on the floor, on our own.

The first camp that responded gave us two different gigs, one at the beginning of summer and one at the end. And from there we pieced together a tour: twenty-five camps across New England. We rehearsed. First with a gig at the Shaker Teen Center, known as P.T.B. (the "place to be"—very cool), where we ironed out the kinks. And then at a community center near my family's summer place in Chautauqua, New York. We were supertight and ready to go.

Versatility was our thing. When we got to a camp we would take requests for the gig that night. We could play it all. A typical lineup would go from Run-DMC's version of "Walk This Way" to the Bee Gees' "Stayin' Alive" to "Parents Just Don't Understand" by DJ Jazzy Jeff & The Fresh Prince to "You Give Love a Bad Name" by Bon Jovi to "Don't You Forget About Me" by Simple Minds. We had no "sound." We'd even throw in our own rockin' versions of camp songs like "If I Had a Hammer."

Experience was our teacher on the road. We learned that slow songs, even Pink Floyd's "Wish You Were Here," killed the magic if it wasn't a camp where the boys and girls wanted to slow dance. Like camps with only boys, for example. We also learned that it didn't take too much to drive the kids crazy. Most had never seen a live band before so they treated us as if we were rock gods. Admittedly, some gigs were justifiably brilliant performances. Camp Meadowbrook was our Budokan. That night we were rocking out. We put an inspired run of songs together—"Joy to the World," "Twist and Shout," then "Prove My Love" by the Violent Femmes. During our version of "Rio" by Duran Duran, it felt like the instruments were playing themselves; we rose above the music and we were just four good friends onstage connecting on a higher plane.

Going back to camp so much older was mind-blowing. Seeing other camps was even more so. I realized just how lazy and disorganized our camp was. There were camps in which programming, athletics, and even survival skills actually occurred. There were also different types of camp directors—from the überdisciplinarian who spent the evening making sure the kids did not get out of their seats, to the old hippies who gave me detailed critiques of how I misplayed the drums on Zeppelin's "Rock and Roll."

But the most critical lesson we learned was about the exclusionary nature of camp—that each camp is an entire universe that outsiders can visit but never become part of. We began the tour with visions of hooking up with different hot counselors every night. It never happened. We had forgotten that every camp was a closed world that we were just passing through. We were doomed to be always at the periphery. Or maybe we were just too dorky. And so every night, once the gig ended and the hall cleared out, we found ourselves alone, sleeping on a stage under the drum kit. I remember waking up in the mornings, thinking for a moment I was in bed at home, then realizing that instead I was in a cold, damp, poorly constructed camp building sleeping on a hard floor next to three of my friends. By choice. And I had to get up and eat some crappy food, teach the kids how to play "New Year's Day" by U2, pack up the van, and hit the road. Another night, another camp. The life of a traveling rock star. I probably should have stayed at home.

THE ROCKIN' KNIGHTS OF SUMMER

DAVID WAIN, PRESIDENT

NEW SUMMER ADDRESS:
19401 South Park Blvd.
Shaker Heights, Ohio 44122
(216) 932-9191

Winter Address (before May 10):
55 E. 10th St. #1101
New York, NY 10003
(212) 614-0320

The summer is filling up fast!! The ROCKIN' KNIGHTS OF SUMMER are almost booked for July and August of 1989, however, there are dates available. Don't deprive your campers of the Rockin' evening activity and morning workshop that will be the hit of scores of camp programs all over Maine, New Hampshire and Vermont. Contact us before it's too late to reserve your date on the tour!

The Rockin' Knights of Summer are college students and former camp counselors from Shaker Heights, Ohio: Scott Harbert--guitar, vocal, keyboard. Dan Kamionkowski--keyboard, guitar, vocal. Steve Kelly--bass, vocal. David Wain--Drums, vocal.

This was a poolside rock 'n' roll extravaganza—note my Pretenders' *Learning to Crawl* '83 tour shirt, which I rarely took off.

David Wain (quote), Steven Kelly (photographer/bass player), Rockin' Knights of Summer oh my #1's you are ... the ecentric wife and #2 K you the husband. well i think i think

your ... shes a ... cow looking really cute 8+ your kinking I Advies, for your house

SUPER GIRL cute I cant beleive I'm doing for well

brovaht out that your up riot. course back x split x well kid

But H found out like this make etc beniene as soup eating your day

Just True stop lied ont a lies, was your day cute kitso

socks (socks) go 90 lied ont 458 choop your soup really cut

this ... think y Rue LLU Pld kid house a

Poop when sees you in ... min ...

PS N/B

Wish You Were Here

"How I wish, how I wish you were here
We're just two lost souls living in a fishbowl, year after year"
—Pink Floyd

Roll over, Rilke, and for that matter, all those who still yearn for the "good old days before e-mail killed the art of letter writing." If ever one needs proof that these folks are all deluded romantics, look no further than that unique genre of literature, the camp letter, which was a weekly (or in some extreme cases, daily) requirement. For most girls, the medium was the message. The content of their letters was far less important than the stationery they so carefully selected, the brand, color, and glitteriness of the pen chosen to create the masterpiece, and the amount of time and energy they devoted to the loopy cursive of the calligraphy. Most boys were literary minimalists. For them, the creative challenge lay in how to fill the empty space of the page with as few words as possible and still make Mom happy. The answer in most cases lay in executing a huge signature, or an artful illustration. The real content most often lay in the P.S.: a short, detailed list of demands for goods, candies, or Def Leppard cassette tapes to be sent from home.

Stacy Bass
Pierce Camp Birchmont
Wolfeboro, NH
1978

123

You were allowed a call from home once a week. You would get a slip while you were eating: "David Lubliner, line one." There were five phones in a line, like in a prison. It was always your mom on the other end. To this day, I believe that these calls were tapped or taped. Too many times a counselor would come up to you right afterward and say, "We know you have a problem, why don't we discuss it . . ."

David Lubliner, Camp Tomahawk, Bristol, NH

Julie Schoenberg, you have a package. You can pick it up at your head counselor's cabin at 12:30 p.m.

Beth

My parents would summer in a beach house at the Jersey shore. The postman would alter his route every day so my mother could get my letter first. She would open it and start crying. And phone my dad, who would drive up from work and ask why he was paying so much for this camp experience when all it did was make his daughter cry and his wife sob all day.

Katie Weinberg Schumacher, French Woods, Hancock, NY

Once a week was mail day—a time to write home and show that you were still alive and not being molested. I discovered how to buck the system one summer when I realized they did not check the letter. They just checked the envelope. I thought I was so smart. Every week I just mailed home empty envelope after empty envelope. One day my mother sent me a package—a rare treat in camp akin to receiving a box of cigarettes in prison. After appropriately showing off the yellow package slip, I picked up the box—and, yes, it was huge. My bunk mates gathered around. The excitement was palpable. I opened the package only to find it was totally empty. My mother had got her own back and one-upped me.

David Light, Camp Ramah in the Poconos, Lake Como, PA

All the kids waited in a long line for their two minutes—a time limit that was strictly policed by the other kids in line. I would get on the phone and start sobbing. Sobbing so hard I couldn't get the words out. The kids behind me had no patience for this. And after two minutes they would start tutting and tapping their watches. I would hang up and slink off. All I had time to do in my two minutes was sob. I never got a word out.

Katie Weinberg Schumacher, French Woods, Hancock, NY

Dear Berna,

wolf - wolf - woof - bark -
pant - slop - few! bark - paw - woof - wolf -
bark.

Tell mommy to give you
a bone. There are three Golden Retrievers
at my sam. One goes horsebackriding
with me. We also have 4 pups
at my camp. They are all cute
and friendly, but I like you the
best.

Dave

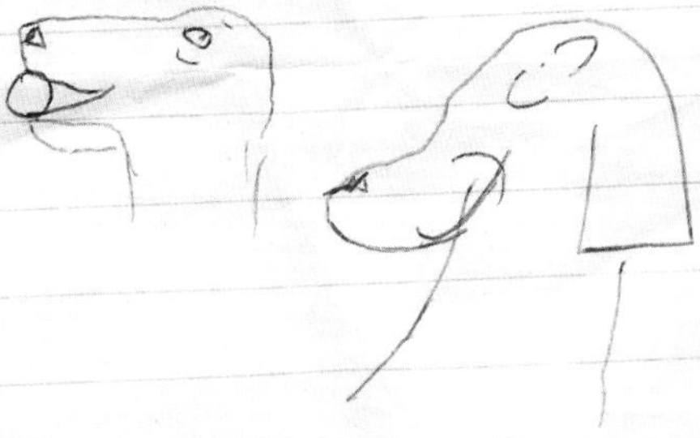

Mom —

Give Berna a bone for
and Please pet + praise her

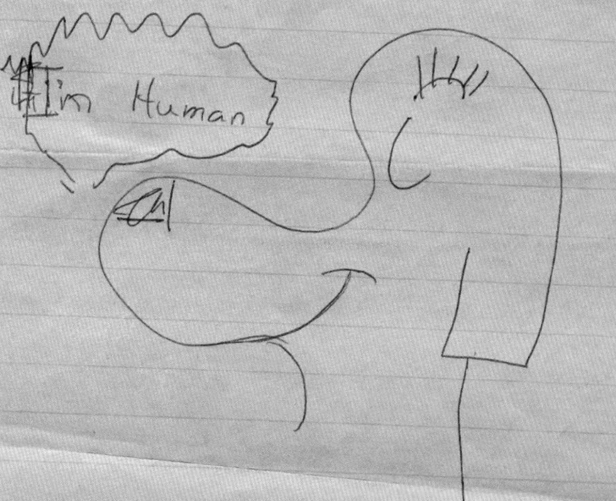

I'm Human

Queen - Freddy Mercury

Sun. June 28

Dear David,

How do you like this postcard? It was a toss-up between this and Elvis, so since this is your current musical favorite – it's yours. You should have seen the ones (DAD) with the ladies when you move the camera. (my they are wearing different clothes - Em)

Just had lunch – it seems like we're always eating – I'm sure we'll be on diets when we get home. Daddy is not fat (yet) [don't believe a thing mommy says] (DAD)

It's a lovely area here – we are on our way to Bergamo! In Italy, everything sounds good, looks good & tastes good.

Keep having fun! Love, Mom & Dad

CR-0140

Printed in Italy

© EDIPOSTERS - Riproduzione...

DAVID SAX
c/o CAMP WALDEN
R.R. 2
PALMER RAPIDS, ONT.

CANADA

ZODAC

QUEEN

FREDDY MERCURY

David Sax
Camp Walden
Palmer Rapids, ON
Canada
1992

for your questions about aids —
I wouldn't worry about Mosquitos.
The research indicates the only known
ways of contracting AIDS, are:
sexual contact ^with an HIV infected person, transmission of
~~the~~ bodily fluids with same and
though blood transfusions of contaminated
blood. I hope this alleviates
your concern.

Lil, by the time you
receive this letter, it will probably
be your last week of camp. I
hope it will be as good for
you as the preceding 7 weeks.
I can't wait to see you again.
Oh, I loved, love
your poem.
(Really good
imagery!)

Dear Mark,

Just wanted
to keep in touch!

Love,
Mom

Mark Miller
Camp Seneca Lake, Honesdale, PA
c. 1984

128

Just wanted you
to know.

Love,
Mom

COUNSELORS

Big Shot

> "You had to have the last word, last night
> You know what everything's about"
> —Billy Joel

Camp may have been been a time of individual freedom to learn about your strengths and weaknesses and test your mind and body in ways you never dreamed were possible, but let's not get too carried away. The average camper was as impressionable as a member of Heaven's Gate, and at every camp there was one counselor who was the teenage equivalent of Marshall Applewhite—the man or woman who all the members of the opposite sex wanted to get with, and all the others wanted to be.

Camp was made for the counselors. Their camaraderie and rule making defined the culture of everyday life. Their word was law and their influence total. The advice they freely dispensed about what to wear, how to act, and who to make out with felt like it was based on vast reservoirs of life experience. Somehow they always seemed to know what was on your mind, perhaps because as recently as a year ago many had been ill-behaved campers themselves and so knew all the tricks of camp life.

Above all, campers were obsessed with the private lives of the counselors. They dreamt of the day they too could enter the magic world of nights off at the local bar, which they learned about when their counselors talked drunkenly to each other as if they were alone after staggering back to the bunk late at night. The campers would listen to every graphic detail as if they were privy to one of the most enthralling human dramas in the world. Even though they barely understood what was being discussed, their young minds absorbed every word, in the hope they could decode them together in the morning and learn all the secrets of beer, weed, and hickeys.

Adam Wallach
Camp Ramah in the
Berkshires
Wingdale, NY
1983

131

1977

When I started, the counselors were immersed in a hippie era. I was from Paterson, New Jersey, where there were race riots going on. I would get letters from my parents about the riots and buildings that were burning, or about the fate of Reuben Carter, who had once eaten dinner at my house. The camp counselors were a total antidote to this with their peace and love vibe. They colored my world and replaced my parents, at least for the summer. They seemed to me like gods that walked the earth. We idolized them. I only had sisters at home. The counselors were my big brothers.

Two in particular stood out. Manny Toonkle was a great athlete. He also had notebooks full of short stories and poems. He was the first counselor to do the long hair and beard combination, so he had a Jesus aura about him. He had that kind of mystery. He was really into music, so in turn, we were all really into music. He turned us all on to Dylan. He made Dylan quotes a currency—"Jeez, I can't find my knees," or "stuck in side of Mobile with the Memphis blues again." They meant nothing to us. We were ten. The only thing we knew was that this was a righteous guy, and he was so cool, I even tried to walk like him. Manny had an alter ego—a ying to his yang. . . . Steve Hanft. He was more the wild and crazy guy . . . his attitude was "life is short; camp is shorter—let's have all the fun we can possibly have." Let's go and raid the girls' bunk —in the middle of the day! Let's take it to the limit. Let's play nude volleyball. He was the one who instilled in us a sense that anything was possible if you were willing to try something different.

People always ask me what the best training is for a job like mine. I always say, become a camp counselor. If you can get forty eight-year-olds to get out of bed, brush their teeth, put on their bathing suits, and follow you down to the waterfront at nine in the morning, you can do anything.

Doug Herzog, Camp Scatico, Elizaville, NY
1977

They were counselors

These were the counselors in my unit that summer. The woman on the bottom right (red shirt) was the camp director's wife, which made being caught on a raid that much worse.

Hillary Auster, Camp Edward Isaacs, Holmes, NY
1987

Looking back, our coolest counselors were all lesbians, though we were oblivious for the longest time and just idolized anyone who wore an ankle bracelet, Birkenstocks, and sported a mullet with a rattail. Then our senior counselor ran off with the head of sports while we were on an overnight trip and a whole world of relationships fell into place. Our head counselor was three hundred pounds of woman who ran camp with an iron fist. She was stern and tough, but could be caring if you were homesick or had a head full of lice. She was the perfect combination of a father figure and a mother figure rolled into one.

Dana Kroll, Camp Walden, Denmark, ME

We were obsessed with the private lives of the counselors. The relationships, the hookups, the breakups, and the antics and partying that went down at the bar they went to . . . the Mountain View, which we all dreamed of one day attending . . . their lives were like soap operas that ran all summer.

Jenny Weiner, Camp Emerson, Hinsdale, MA

Julie Jacobs
Camp Lochearn
Post Mills, VT
1983

One minute you are a camper in a bunk with your best friends. Then the next you are sixteen—separated and spread out throughout the bunks. In part, it felt like our lives were over. Like we would never see each other again. But on the other hand, we also had a real sense of responsibility and of giving back to camp. But we were so young to have this responsibility thrust upon us, to watch kids 24/7 for two straight months, with no skills and little support. We were thrown in at the deep end. To cope with ADD they gave us a one-page fact sheet and that constituted our training!

Rachel Kane, Camp Che-Na-Wah, Minerva, NY

Was it that our training was so bad? Or that our camp was so bad in general? Or was it just that the whole of America was like that at this time? We would take bunk trips on a winding road in the back of an open truck with no lights, driven by a drunk driver, with the kids hanging on for dear life while trying to make out at the same time. All this to get to Dairy Queen.

Michael Wolfson, Camp Boiberik, Rhinebeck, NY

By nature I was very shy and less engaged as a camper. As a counselor I had to fight this and try to change. When else do you get the chance to be so self-aware and to play a role that other people, other kids, could aspire to?

Jon Steingart, Camp Hess Kramer, Malibu, CA

I was made a counselor at sixteen. I was the first to admit I was not equipped to be supervising children. What was our training? Half an hour to run through the list of kids to note which ones had ADD, which were bed wetters, which were on Ritalin. The rest of the two-day precamp orientation consisted of fixing the place up—picking up oversize sticks and removing them. We had no clue about the kids and could cope with very little in terms of control. One summer the kids got lice. All of them. We had to wash their hair with lice-killing shampoo. We did not know you had to keep it out of their eyes. Our kids had to wear BluBlockers for weeks.

Andrew Goldberg, Camp Wildwood, Bridgton, ME

Pinemere Camp 1991

I was made a unit head when I was eighteen years old. I had seventy-five kids under me and was running a staff of fifteen. I was responsible for shaping campers' lives, tackling their problems, and brokering deals with their parents. I did not know any better, so I never questioned that an entire universe was at my command.

Lauren Stein
Camp Pinemere
Stroudsburg, PA
1991

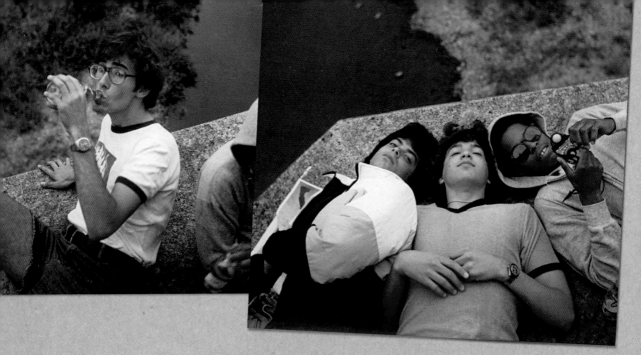

Hanging out on our day off drinking Genesee beer on an abandoned railroad bridge, or at least what we thought was an abandoned railroad bridge.

Doug Grad, French Woods, Hancock, NY
1980

Woody's Tavern was the greatest place to spend a night off, bar none. I loved to drink, and Woody the owner would serve you $1 pitchers of Killian's Red as long as you had a note from your mother saying you were twenty-one. I learned to drink there. To do shots. I drank more there than at any time in my life. And the miracle was, you loved camp so much that you got up with no hangover—just with delight and pleasure and ready to do it again. Woody's was an orgy. By the end of the night we would all be in the parking lot hooking up. At two we would all run back to camp, zipping up our pants on the way.

    The locals hated us. There were some classic fights until Woody realized that the campers were his cash cow and started catering to us, going so far as to develop promotional packages of pitchers and T-shirts.

Brad Feldman, Camp Greylock, Becket, MA

When your counselors had the night off, the trick was to get them to bring you back food. You would go to sleep at lights-out safe in the knowledge that you had given $6 to a counselor and that soon a pepperoni pizza, chocolate shake, and a Fribble from Friendly's would be on its way to you. You would sleep sweetly knowing that you were going to be woken up with a hot pizza and a cold milkshake, which you would gobble in the darkness and then go right back to sleep.

Scott Jacoby, Camp Greylock, Becket, MA

At the age of about nine or ten, I was hanging around with the fourteen- to fifteen-year-old kids and heard one call another a "douchebag." I had never heard this word and didn't know what it meant, but I liked the way it sounded and began to use the word as frequently as possible among my own cabin mates. When one of our counselors heard me calling other kids "douchebags," he asked if I knew what it meant. I responded negatively. He told me, "You should never use a word if you don't know what it means."

"So, what does it mean?" I asked.

He said, "OK, everybody gather round," and told us the following:

A lot of athletes, but especially professional football players, undergo a special operation so they can remove their testicles during a game to make sure that when they get hit in the balls it doesn't hurt. What the operation does is to insert a special snap, kind of like the ones on your pajamas, on the upper part of the ball sac, so the players can snap their balls on and off easily. When they play a game, they keep their balls in a special bag, which is called a "douchebag."

Not only did we believe this guy, but because we were at an age during which we were constantly giving each other wedgies and hitting each other in the nuts, we all wanted to get the "douchebag operation." We ran all over the camp telling the other kids about how we were all going to get "douchebags for our balls." One kid even wrote a letter to his parents asking if he could get the "douchebag operation" when he got home. The camp director subsequently received a phone call from an irate and confused father demanding to know what his son was learning at camp and why his son was so interested in douchebags.

But by the time the director came over to us to inquire about the famed "douchebag" procedure, we had already been informed by some of the older kids that we had been duped by our counselor and that a douchebag was, in fact, not a sterile bag where one kept one's testicles during a sporting event, but something to do with vaginal cleansing.

Imagine our disappointment.

Somewhat dejected, our desire for douchebags quickly disappeared. But the word remained an integral part of our lexicon, for some of us to this very day.

Eddy Portnoy, Camp Tomahawk, Bristol, NH

Tom Rosenberg
Camp Scatico, Elizaville, NY
c. 1978

THE NATURE OF MY NURTURE

BY ALEX GROSSMAN

I was a camp counselor for seven days. Eight if you count the five hours I clocked on the day I was fired, but as my so-called severance check revealed, the camp's bean counters clearly did not believe in prorating. My journey of disgrace from camp in Pennsylvania to my parents' cabin in northern Michigan took eleven hours. I did it straight through, pushing both my silver Escort GT and the number of times any nineteen-year-old can enjoy Ace of Base's "All That She Wants" to the limit.

Why was I booted after only one week? Was I truly a bad counselor? Absolutely. But it was more than that. I never had a chance. I had been conditioned to suck. My Pavlovian fall was set in motion many years earlier at Camp Tamarack in Ortonville, Michigan. I was twelve, the year was 1983, and the nationwide ban on rattails and atomic wedgies wasn't even a whisper in a neurotic Jewish mother's mouth. It was here at Camp Tamarack that I learned "the rules" of the camper-counselor relationship, which in this case was as close to that of feudal lord and serf as current state laws would tolerate. As campers, we fulfilled one and only one purpose—to amuse our counselors. Our seasonal survival was based solely on our ability (both innate and learned) to entertain, serve, and feed our fickle and perversely creative masters' minds. If there was a benevolent old king of the camp, I never met him, and he certainly never intervened on our peasantly behalf.

Hyperbole, you say? Mellifluously flowery and metaphorical? Absolutely. Yet it's all true! Perhaps it's better if I let the following list speak for itself:

I Before *E* Except After *C*: My bunk mates and I were routinely blindfolded and locked in cramped, confined spaces for hours on end. Hungry, thirsty, and scared to death, we were forced to listen to a loop of the same maddening Yaz song, "*I* Before *E* Except after *C*," until one of us either cracked, peed our pants, or both.

This looks like a meeting of the North American Man/Boy Love Association, but it is actually me meeting my counselor for the first time.

Alex Grossman
Camp Tamarack, Ortonville, MI
1983

Night of a Thousand Stars: After a feast of hearty drink and fine sinse-milla, our counselors would stumble into our bunks, armed with glossy eyes, perma-grins, and hundreds of flashlights. Shining the blinding lights in our eyes, they charged us with the impossible task of providing real answers to fictional camp trivia. "Who set the camp record for lake swims in 1972? Steven 'Swim-mer's Ear' Jacobson? No, you fool! Miles 'Aqua-Lung' Berg!"

Exodus: Late one evening, my camp mates and I were rounded up and forced to march together to the lake. As the sun set across the murky waters, we were informed that this evening's performance required us to play the role of European Jews, while counselors, armed with flashlights and halfheartedly camouflaged cans of Pabst Blue Ribbon, would tackle the part of German spies. Beginning on one side of the lake, we "Jews" shoved off in clunky metal canoes, as our counselors took their time jetting after us in sleek, motorized rowboats. If a flashlight shone on your face, it meant you were eliminated, although our tormentors rarely stopped until a canoe had been capsized. Those healthy, speedy ones that reached the other side of the lake then had to race through the woods and total darkness of night back to the other side of camp. Miraculously, after running around scared shitless until dawn and shredding my pants on a ten-foot barbed-wire fence, I was one of only four kids to make it back that summer. I still have the scar on my knee to prove it.

Hiking Is Fun!: This bit began with the counselors loading us into the back of a windowless van. They would drive for what seemed like forever and then drop us off in the middle of dense woods with only a compass, melted Hershey bars, and a few canteens of warm well water. After a few frantic, terrified *Lord of the Flies* hours, we found our bearings and realized we were only a mile or so from camp. Assholes.

Good times, right? Actually, it kind of was. Looking back, I can't say I was ever too disturbed by any of their behavior. I mean, it's not like they physically abused us, and as far as torture goes, this was pretty ingenious stuff. Plus, like all good captor/tormentors, they knew exactly when to slip us a bone. Whether it was a secret midnight delivery of cheeseburgers and soggy fries, or helping us relieve the younger campers of their Pop Rocks and Razzles, they knew precisely when we needed a lift. It's funny, but at the start of each summer, when our oppressors covered our hands with Vaseline and forced us to sort thousands of impossibly small cake sprinkles by color, I knew even then that these were special times. My only question was what inspired these evil geniuses.

As fate would have it, years later as a freshman at the University of Michigan, I would find out. In what I hoped was a choice more subconscious than masochistic, I pledged Sigma Alpha Mu, the exact same fraternity at the exact same university that my adolescent tormentors had pledged almost a decade earlier. And, lo and behold, in a cruel and Sisyphean twist of fate, all the old tortures and afflictions were resumed. From being locked in a stairwell to praying to the skull of a dead and rapidly decaying goat, the details were too similar to be mere coincidence. And then it hit me: My old counselors, also SAM pledges at the time, were suffering through these same hazing rituals! I couldn't believe it. This was a case of transferred aggression so textbook it was clear even to a failing Psych 101 student like myself! Like a member of a Duran Duran fan group, I was both sickened and delighted with the realization that there were others like me.

I was part of a chain. A sick, deprived, juvenile chain, but a chain nonetheless! And isn't that what life's all about? Finding community and continuity in our lives and the lives of others? A sense of belonging? Well, now I had it in spades. To this day my pals and I from the fraternity can still recite the Greek alphabet three times before a match burns out in our trembling hands. Awesome!

Which, believe it or not, brings us back to my expulsion as counselor, and that long car ride home. You see, I wasn't kicked out of camp for anything as cliché as drinking, fighting, or smoking marijuana cigarettes. I was kicked out of camp for, well, behaving like a counselor. Or at least how I thought a counselor was supposed to behave. Aren't campers supposed to be woken up in the middle of the night and forced to march blindfolded through the woods? Shouldn't seven-year-olds learn to forge letters of abandonment from the parents of rival campers? Evidently, Lonnie, one super-sized spoiled youngster, didn't think so. Armed with an extra fifty pounds, a foul Long Island accent, and enough Fila, Ellesse, and Sergio Tacchini warmup outfits to make a tennis pro blush, the little brat ratted me out, and I was promptly dismissed. Political correctness, perhaps correctly, had taken hold of our country and our camps. Hazing and pegged jeans were out, passive-aggressiveness and Timberlands were in. While Lonnie and his gang of merry fatsoes rejoiced at my termination, another group of my campers were left with real tears in their eyes. Even after seven days, they had grown fond of me, much as I had grown fond of my own wardens so many years earlier. Isn't Stockholm Syndrome lovely? And as I traded the foothills of Pennsylvania for Michigan, I smiled to myself, wondering if maybe there was a future frat or two in the bunch. As I rounded the lake into Michigan, the weather grew warmer and I was forced to remove the one material souvenir I had left camp with: a seemingly tailor-made canary yellow and indigo blue Sergio Tacchini warmup suit. Thanks for that, Lonnie. You fat bastard.

Jim Cone
Chase Camp
Westchester, PA
1987

Dear Mom,

My Councler was fired. Please don't Call me up because it will make me homesick just send me stuff like in other various letters I have sent ya

Love, Jim Cone

Camp Mah Kee Nac
Lenox, MA
c. 1985

My bunk (B-11) during a lazy afternoon—on my day off—with all my stuff on the porch. My bunk mates put my whole "area" (bed, cubbies, trunk underneath the bed, etc.) outside as a joke, and took pictures with my camera of people hanging out on my bed.

I totally remember coming back to the bunk that evening and for about ten seconds was not too happy, then thinking, this is kind of funny, and seriously thinking how creative that was, and realizing they had planned this for days.

Adam Wallach,
Camp Ramah, Wingdale, NY
1986

Karen Lauterstein
KenWood Camp, Kent, CT
1989

How to Start a Conversation With A Child

Now what do you do to break the ice and start a conversation? ...
Ask the child a question.

Some ice-breaking questions are good, but others are not-so-good. Not-so-good questions include questions that sting with sarcasm, questions that cause embarrassment, or questions that may remind the child of a fear—especially the fear of being away from home.

Not-So-Good Questions

- "Is that your face, or did somebody barf on your neck?"
- "Did you make any friends on the bus this morning?"
- "Are you glad to be here?"
- "You look skinny: don't your parents feed you?"
- "Do you miss your mom and dad?"
- "Didn't anybody tell you that you're not allowed to bring candy here?"
- "What do you have in that giant suitcase—a dead body?"
- "Hi, I'm Mike, your new counselor. Can I borrow a dollar?"

Prudence Chapman
New London County 4-H Camp
North Franklin, CT
1992

My bunk had a counselor, Scott, who was always with different girls. We would line up before a social and he would inspect us to make sure he liked our outfit. If he did not, he would make us change. We were all pretty much wearing the same thing—a variation on the blue button-down, white pants, lot of gel in the hair. Drakkar was then sprayed in the air and it would descend upon us. He knew all of our plans—who we wanted to hook up with and what we wanted to do—and he would send us out into the night armed with tips on the ways of love for each situation.

Mark Boxer, Camp Watitoh, Becket, MA

Amherst was where we would go on our day off. We used to head for the novelty store Joke City to buy masks to wear for scaring campers. These red-hood-black-mesh beauties were the greatest. Storm into the bunk wearing these in the middle of the night and someone was guaranteed to crap themselves.

Brad Feldman,
Camp Greylock, Becket, MA
1989

My hero was a counselor named Goobie. Jonathan Goldberg. The hottest, strongest, coolest guy ever, he was the Jewish Jim Thorpe. If ever anything needed physical acumen, Goobie was the man. He could take on any counselor from any camp anywhere mano a mano. We knew that if Goobie went down, we all went down. He was our first and last line of defense against the townies of Kresgeville/Kunkletown who would terrorize us after nightfall with their ATVs and pickups, which they would speed around camp in after one a.m. As we listened to their engines, the sounds of them skinny-dipping in our pool, the honking of their horns, them drunk off their asses . . . we were sure our lives were over at the age of thirteen. We would lie awake in our bunks terrified. What was by day a tranquil paradise for horny youths became by night pogromlike conditions. We felt violated. But we stayed close to Goobie. We always knew where he was after dark.

Ross Martin, Camp Harlam, Kresgeville, PA
1988

GALIL UNIT HEAD:
Jon "Goobie" Goldberg

My campers were suburban kids who had never been laid before. They talked a load of bullshit on the subject. One night a kid came back to the bunk at two a.m. and woke me up. He was terrified. He had "gone to the benches" and ended up having sex with a fourteen-year-old camper. This kid had no idea about what he was doing. AIDS was a massive, massive deal. He had no idea whether his condom had worked or not. He had no idea how a condom worked at all. He had it in hand, fully loaded, and wanted me to check it to assure him that it had done its duty.

Mik Moore, Camp Tel Yehudah, Barryville, NY

It was widely believed that Camp Echo Lark was situated down the road from a mental institution. And as legend goes, it housed a serial killer named Hatchet Harry. One rainy night, our counselor ran into our bunk and said that Hatchet Harry had escaped from the mental institution. We were to seal the bunk immediately. Barricade the doors and windows. If he was to penetrate our cabin, we were told to avoid eye contact at all costs. He was like a bear. He only responded to body movement, so if he cornered you *just stay frozen*. The counselors left to patrol the camp and we were on our own. Some cried. Others took action. We organized ourselves into a rotation system, each person keeping a lookout on a different part of the bunk. My watch was the window by the showers. After an hour on guard, a hand slowly reached through the window carrying a hatchet. I literally leapt twenty feet and broke down sobbing. The counselors finally let us in on the joke, told us to go to bed, and called me a girl for crying.

Adam Goldberg, Camp Echo Lark, Poyntelle, PA

World Leader Pretend

"I have been given the freedom
To do as I see fit"
—R.E.M.

For every yin, there is a yang. And just as every camp had a small group of counselors who were perfect in every way, they also had a contingent of foreign counselors from Britain, France, and even Hungary who were the opposite of sex. The importation of foreign counselors was a great racket from the camp's perspective. They could take advantage of victims' hunger to view the workings of the world's supreme superpower up close, paying them slave wages in exchange for a temporary work visa. The Europeans were like sailors lured onto the rocks by sirens. They arrived with grand visions of seeing the America of *Dallas* and *Beverly Hills Cop* up close, only to find themselves quickly dispatched to camps in the backwoods to work as soccer coaches or dishwashers before they knew what had hit them.

Foreign counselors fell into two categories. There were those who quickly adjusted and "got" camp, who were able to adapt to its unique rhythms and could even become sought-after objects of lust, especially if they drove the water-ski motorboat. But there were also those poor souls who never recovered from being sent out to the sticks. They were generally left to band together and serve out their term before being freed to tour the country by Greyhound. They are easy to pick out in photo albums, lurking resentfully around the back of group shots wearing socks with sandals, cutoff denim shorts, tight T-shirts, and plagued with sunburn.

> This look is pure Madchester. I had to take care of a bunk of six-year-olds. I taught them how to box and spent the summer pairing them up and watching them fight. Six-year-olds are great to watch. They can't really hurt each other but on the rare occasion they connect with a punch, it is a thing of beauty.
>
> Michael Cohen
> Camp Louemma
> Sussex, NJ
> 1991

I FELL IN LOVE WITH AN ENGLISH COUNSELOR!!!

BY REBECCA SHAPIRO

You would think that as a Jewish girl from Lincoln Park, Chicago, I would naturally have gravitated toward the Jewish counselors at Camp Walden. Boys like Adam Schecter and Kevin Lakritz—athletic types from suburban Detroit who had Jewish afros and would later be in fraternities at the University of Michigan. But in the summer of 1992, I fell in love with Martyn Jones. Martyn Jones was an English boy brought to me courtesy of the Camp America program, which delivered clueless English students to act as counselors at camps across the U.S. with the promise that they would be free to travel the country together in a ratty car before they had to return to university.

Among the many interesting things I learned at camp was that Jewish women go wild for English counselors. Martyn grew up in a small town called Amesbury, in Salisbury, which he said was near Stonehenge, a fact that made him seem all the more dreamy. I found myself spending my evenings in the local bar, the Pines, huddled in the corner with the English, Scottish, and Irish boys in their uniform of cutoff denims topped off with a New Order or R.E.M. T-shirt. They spent the evenings laughing at the American counselors as they downed too many beers and played Garth Brooks's "Friends in Low Places" over and over on the jukebox. And I laughed along with them. These boys were so different from the ones I knew in Chicago. Hanging out with them made me feel special—maybe it was just the ton of extra attention they sent my way.

Martyn stood out as the epitome of cool. He was so sexy, in a Stone Roses kind of way. He taught windsurfing—what could be more attractive than that? While he demonstrated longboarding techniques to precious little Costa Rican boys named Jacob on the shores of beautiful Long Lake, I was the canoe instructor's assistant. Every day I would make the seven-year-old Latino boys paddle the canoe over to Martyn's windsurfing territory. I would be in my bikini in the center, giving out orders in broken Spanish on the J-stroke, and Martyn would laugh. We first bonded over a mutual love for the House of Love, a noisy, electric pop outfit from England fronted by the sweet-voiced lead singer Guy Chadwick, who had chiseled cheekbones, sunken eyes, and an ability to churn out the darkest of lyrics. The first clue Martyn liked me was that he spent an increasing amount of time down at the Pines serenading me on his guitar with the House of Love songs "I Don't Know Why I Love You" and "Shine On." My confidence was reinforced the day his best friend, David, a bloated bloke from Edinburgh, approached me with the magic words "Martyn wants to get off with you." Pretty soon we were spending all our free time together. Walden gave us one day off a week so I would always try to coordinate my day off with Martyn's, and several of us would pile into someone's station wagon and spend the day at the beach, topped off by a trip to Dairy Queen, where we would order an extra-large vanilla frozen yogurt shake with blueberry and rainbow sprinkles, or hiking at the Sleeping Bear Dunes near Traverse City.

The author and
Martyn Jones
Camp Walden
Cheboygan, MI
1992

This truly magical summer ended and we decided we were still very much in love, so Martyn persuaded his pale, pasty friends to make a detour on their cross-country journey and visit me at my school, Connecticut College. He pulled into New London in a battered secondhand station wagon. I was ecstatic. The four days we spent together were perhaps the best of my college years. I put Martyn's friends David and Gerard in an empty dorm room and Martyn and I took over my room. When I was at class or cross-country practice, Martyn would sit cross-legged on my floor, using my portable tape player to make me a mix tape with all his music. He made two of them and I can still recite every song on the cassettes. I used to spend the weeks after he left analyzing their lyrics, trying to piece together exactly what it was he meant to say to me. Ride, Lush, the Blue Airplanes, R.E.M., That Petrol Emotion, the La's, Catherine Wheel, Billy Bragg,

On the cassette insert (TDK D60):

A. NOISE REDUCTION ☐ON ☐OFF

Cool Grooves — MARTYN

That Petrol Emotion – Sensitize
Teenage Fanclub – The Concept
(Live) The House Of Love – Destroy
The Heart, Can't Stand It,
Philly Phile, The Blue Aeroplanes
– Jacket Hangs, Your Ages,
Cud – Crash a Buzz.
Ian McCulluch – Cool song

B. DATE/TIME
NOISE REDUCTION ☐ON ☐OFF

Revolver – Earth You Have
Boo Radleys – Sunset
Charlatans – Chewing Gum
Weekend Ride – Twisterella
Mouse Trap, Time Machine
Electronic

---

the Wonderstuff, Massive Attack, James—I had better taste in music than all my friends.

I spent the entire fall semester plotting my next trip to visit Martyn. Over the Christmas holiday my parents had planned a family vacation to Paris and London, and I decided to take the train up to Manchester, where Martyn would pick me up at the station and whisk me away to Crewe and Alsager College. There we would fool around in bed for ten blissful days, staring longingly into each other's eyes. But this was not to be. Somewhere between New London and Crewe and Alsager, Martyn had decided that he was "no longer in love with me, that there was no point in trying to continue a relationship with an American, blah blah." Unfortunately, he had neglected to inform me of his change of thinking prior to my visit so I arrived young and naive and pink-cheeked and left a bloated, sad, miserable wreck. We spent the first four days at his student digs in Crewe near Manchester. There was barely any running water in the house, let alone heat, and he would barely kiss me. I look back at photos from this time and I see myself wearing a thick black leather coat and I have no idea what I was thinking, since it was so unflattering. I never took it off, though. I spent my time watching Martyn and his roommates eating fish and chips and some Indian meat that I never caught the name of. While they sat around, watched TV, and debated the merits of Kylie Minogue and her ass, I cried myself to sleep.

Fast-forward fifteen years: I am now a music publicist who is very passionate about what she does. Though my love for music developed in my early teens, a little bit of Martyn Jones lives on in my appreciation of the British music scene, stretching my taste beyond Depeche Mode and Erasure. My knowledge of British artists from the early to mid-'90s runs deep. While I can't say too much about Mavis Staples and the Staple Singers without prior research, I can still talk all night about Guy Chadwick, the Cure pre-"Just Like Heaven," and even "Friends in Low Places."

HUNGARIAN STAFF

Gabor Nagy and Barr
Kantor

Our shower house was the most disgusting place on earth. Everyone knew to wear flip-flops in there. Everyone, apart from the foreign counselors. Every year one of them would walk in there barefoot, guaranteed. We reacted with such shock at this you would think he had AIDS or something.

Brad Feldman, Camp Greylock, Becket, MA

Simon Poulter was a counselor one summer. He studied at Leeds and won me over with his *FRANKIE SAYS RELAX!* T-shirt. He was nineteen. I was thirteen. He worked the waterfront. At flag raising, the whole camp would line up from the youngest to the oldest. For me it was the time to stare at the boy you liked. And I could not take my eyes off him. I started to hang out with him while he swept the mess hall during tribe time. It took me all summer to make him notice me. But one night, during a raid, he came to my bunk, tickled me awake, and we stayed up all night chatting. On the last night, Simon was guarding the younger kids' bunks. Just standing there. I crept up to him and just went for it. He was shocked. I was thirteen and I just jumped him. He came back to camp the next year. But by then I was going out with Ricky Epstein, who sent me letters soaked in Ralph Lauren cologne.

Amy Israel, Camp Watitoh, Becket, MA

His name was Skunk. And he was from just outside Liverpool, where they breed them big and Gold's Gym was still a booming business.

Deb Gitell
Camp Kingswood
Bridgton, ME
1990

DIRECTORS AND STAFF

My Prerogative

"Oh oh oh I don't need permission
Make my own decisions"
—Bobby Brown

Most camp directors' career choices were based on the simple fact that they loved their own experiences as campers so much that they basically never left. Camp sessions were the golden days of their adolescent experience, and so they entered the business, only to discover that the promise of eternal youth in Peter Pan is just a myth. Being a camper may have been daily doses of bunk camaraderie and masturbation. But being a camp director is all about dealing with leaky roofs, chronic bed wetters, frantic parents, and bank deficits—a deadly foursome designed to wipe the smile off anyone's face.

How the camp director adjusted to this new reality determined the kind of leader they would be. There were those who relied on the security of the whistle around the neck and clipboard in hand as a desperate claim to the authority they never truly established. And then were those who grew into the role, becoming the kind of feared and beloved leader who personifies the traditions, values and motto of the camp itself. These charismatic types, who knew every trick in the book, could silence a room with their mere presence, or make a camper's summer with a few quiet words of praise. Their well-worn life stories, rife with tales of war heroism or great sporting achievement, shaped the lives of thousands of campers, whether they were true or not.

But no director, no matter how charismatic, made the magic happen alone. They were field marshals for an army of counselors, janitors, handymen, nurses, cooks, and laundry workers whom we also salute in the following pages, despite the fact they are as motley looking a-crew as could be assembled outside of a Texas prison chain gang.

Bill is an absolute legend. He was as likely to pass the sagest nugget of grandfatherly wisdom on to you during a chat at the pool as he was to moon your grandmother on Visiting Day.

Matthew Rosen
Lake Owego Camp
Greeley, PA
1992

LAUNDRY

Brandon and Sunni ran the laundry, which was on top of a hill. You would look up and see them walking around wearing your clothes. I would see them in my Wisconsin sweatshirt. Did you go to Wisconsin, Sunni?

Brad Feldman, Camp Greylock, Becket, MA
1988

Camp was a Ritalin vacation. A time parents would experiment with easing their kids off Ritalin. Kids would be flying off the walls. Three times a day the line for Ritalin would be massive. The nurses were like drug dealers.

Simmy Kunstavitz, Camp Ramah in the Berkshires, Wingdale, NY

The infirmary doled out Bengay for everything. We had an outbreak of salmonella one summer. Kids were dropping like flies. They did not know what to give us, they were so not prepared. The best they could do was to hand out Pepto and water to us all.

Lauren Stein, Camp Pinemere, Stroudsburg, PA

There were four camp directors, all of whom were gym teachers or principals, though it was never clear to me how any could pass for either. One of them founded the camp in what felt like 1809, and she died when I was in my early teens. She was sort of like the Queen of England with three Tony Blairs who actually ran the place. What I remember most about her was she had animals stuffed and mounted in the room where she slept and she was rarely seen without an unfriendly, pearl necklace–wearing poodle named Misty. All of the directors, young and old, used to tool around the camp in golf carts, with the younger campers running behind them clamoring for a ride as if these carts were UN supply trucks in an impoverished nation. The cart drivers were happy to share this perk, for the most part. Unless there was some urgent camp business and the golf cart could not afford to be weighed down by eighty-pound prepubescent stick bugs. In which case we got a "sorry, girls" and the carts zoomed on. I couldn't imagine what could be so urgent—explosives in the lake? a maintenance man with kiddie porn?—none of it seemed realistic. I guess with small golf carts comes the idea of great responsibility. It was probably a bat in the mess hall.

Sloane Crossley, Camp Wa-klo, Keane, NH

One of our maintenance men had a treble clef chin. He had a son called Cub. He was a recovering alcoholic who drank a lot. In fact, he made his own moonshine. He had been a roadie for Aerosmith and would fire rifles on his property in the middle of the night, but he was six feet, five inches and 300 pounds so no one argued too much. Jay the bathroom guy was covered in navy tattoos. He had a big bushy handlebar mustache he referred to as his "womb broom." He worshipped Apollo Creed. He spent his evenings trying to catch us raiding, and when he did he would shout out, "You'd better watch it, you are messing with the Master of Disaster." We bought him a case of Bud and left it on his steps. We never had any problems with him again.

Andrew Goldberg, Camp Wildwood, Bridgton, ME

Camp Ramah
Ojai, CA
c. 1987

Walter skating. This guy was a dishwasher but an eccentric one. He roller-skated every day and flew model airplanes.

Doug Herzog, Camp Scatico, Elizaville, NY
c. 1979

Henry Hacker was the greatest man that ever lived. He looked like Alan Greenspan and was a people person running a sports camp. He had never married, had no kids of his own, but he made a point of kissing every kid good night every night. It felt like the greatest honor in the world when he came into your bunk at night and asked you to hold his lantern. On Sundays, after we got to sleep in, we would get together and eat donuts from Dunkin'. Henry would dole out orange juice from a huge industrial pot. We would all line up to get it and as he poured it into your cup he would name your zip code. That's how well he knew us.

Anonymous, Camp Cedar, Casco, ME

SOME THOUGHTS FROM TED

Singing and camp have gone together since I first started my own camping days. At its best, group singing represents the unity, spirit, fun, friendship, and just plain feeling good that the "sing-song" experience gives to so many campers and staff each summer.

Since the first days of Walden, back in the summer of 1970, we have been a singing camp. Our campers and staff have always looked forward to the various types of sing-songs and serious concerts that I've done with them during their stay at camp.

I believe that singing is as important to the over-all camp program as any other activity. I also believe that young people should be exposed to as many different kinds of music as possible. With these beliefs firmly entrenched, I will continue to expand my own repertoire as well as teaching and introducing lots of new songs and music to Walden.

The seeds of this record were planted many years ago by any number of our Walden family. They thought it would be a great idea to have a recording of a sing-song as one of their camp memories.

HERE IT IS — done in one take only, with all its spirit, enthusiasm, serious moments, misplaced microphones, broken banjo strings, singing off key, clapping, whistling, shouting, singing too quickly (or playing too slowly) and a just plain good time.

To those of you who will be coming to Walden for the first time; here is an opportunity to learn some of our songs before you arrive at camp. For those who have been coming to Walden for years, or are former campers, here are a few more memories for you to hold onto.

LET'S SING OUT

Ted Cole, the director, was a huge folk music fan. His cabin was filled with records, and he introduced hundreds of campers to Bob Dylan's music each summer. The singsongs on the first night were his legendary way of initiating the new and stirring up the old. But they could also be political. Older campers came to realize that a spontaneous singsong in the dining hall after lunch was a delaying tactic by Ted to mask the fact that a staff member had been fired and had an hour to pack and get out of camp. The singsong was usually reserved for the one or two mass firings per summer, when Ted would clear out a few staff at once while avoiding messy tears or kids pleading with the head staff not to let their favorite counselor go. Whenever he'd whip out a guitar after grilled cheese, staff and older campers quickly looked around to see who was missing.

David Sax, Camp Walden, Palmer Rapids, ON, Canada
1990

Shrubs the woodwork counselor was an icon. A Jew who could do something with his hands. He was a real hero and made being on theater crew the thing to be.

Michael Wolfsohn, Camp Boiberik, Rhinebeck, NY

Nigel Bennett
Camp Kingswood
Bridgton, ME
1986

Eight out of ten camp directors claim to be an Olympic record holder. Our camp director, Arie Gluck, claimed to be an Israeli silver medalist or a bronze medal winner—it always changed. We assumed he meant the Maccabiah games and not the Olympics but that was unclear. His best friend and right-hand man was Raffi, who was also, coincidentally, an Olympic medal holder. Raffi toggled between being the director of sports, the chief of maintenance, and the tech guy—a role which he took really seriously. He was forever carting the camp's primitive speaker system around. You would be halfway through a cold-water stream hike, and you would emerge from the water in the middle of nowhere and there he would be, calmly setting up those two giant speakers to a generator for an impromptu talent show.

Ross Martin, Camp Harlam, Kresgeville, PA

Gary Wilensky was our tennis counselor—a larger-than-life figure who would come onto court in roller skates and in drag. We had T-shirts that said GARY'S GIRLS. We left camp one summer and he was all over television and even on *Inside Edition*. He had kidnapped someone he taught and the police chased him to a dungeon lair where he shot himself dead wearing one of his drag outfits. All the props we had found so cute were found in the lair.

Anonymous, Tripp Lake Camp, Poland, ME

Al Jaworski, the seventy-year-old swim instructor, was my nemesis. Al was the head of waterfront. He had two dogs, Trixie and Tasha. His signature look was tight shorts and a *Gilligan's Island* hat. He put his decades of experience to work to ensure that swimming was no fun whatsoever. At camp, I was a Raider. Raiding was my thing. I rounded up forty of my best bunk mates and surrounded Al's shack in the middle of the night, banging the sides so hard we made his stuff fall off the shelves. Al's pride and joy was his planter, which he tended to with love and care. I snapped off a flower and put it on his doorstep covered in ketchup with a note attached that warned, "You're Next Old Man."

Andrew Goldberg, Camp Wildwood, Bridgton, ME

REMEMBRANCE OF A CAMP DIRECTOR PAST: DAVID ADLER

BY STUART BLUMBERG

The first tough Jew I ever met was my camp director David Adler. Ex-Israeli Army, David moved to America in his twenties, married a beautiful young Jewess, and took over the camp her family had run for decades. My first year as a camper in 1980 was his second as camp director. Meeting David made me realize something: most young Jewish boys don't grow up wanting to be Albert Einstein or Alan Greenspan. They want to be Barney Ross, Sandy Koufax, Goldberg the wrestler, or Bugsy Siegel. They want to be what their cultural imperative denies them: namely, badasses.

David was so unlike the nebbishy, sedentary Semites of my Cleveland youth, the men who never seemed to take risks outside of their portfolio allocations. David was a doer, a man intimately attuned to his physical self. Over 6 feet and 220 pounds, with a voice so deep and commanding he made Paul Robeson sound like Richie Cunningham, David struck us as literally larger than life.

He had that thing—the infectious charisma thing. People wanted to be around David, to bask in his resounding laughs and freely given bear hugs, to feel the bristles of his beard tickle their necks. On the flip side, David had a mean temper. He was known to break glasses when angry, to cuss disturbingly when you messed up, to fix you with a stare so scary your balls ran for cover. Still, we were willing to risk Daddy David's ire as long as we could bask in the hearth fire of his good moods. As you have probably gathered, the man oozed contradiction. One day, he would wear Israeli battle fatigues, the next he would show up to a breakfast dressed only in a woman's evening robe. David enjoyed nothing more than defying easy categorization. Part Ari Ben Canaan, part David Bowie, the

160

man marched to a very unorthodox drummer.

The man also oozed power. A black belt in Shotokan karate, David not only insisted the camp have its own karate dojo complete with Japanese master, but that all campers participate in compulsory weekly training. In David's eyes, martial arts were a crucible from which young souls could emerge into their more disciplined, self-confident beingdom. It is thanks to David that I know how to count from one through ten in Japanese: "*Ich, Ni, San, Chi, Go, Ro . . .*" I will never forget the way he looked practicing kata, his gut hanging out between the flaps of his immaculate white *gi,* or the way he would scream "Keeyaii!" while breaking a board at one of his many karate demonstrations.

David Adler as shot by the author
Camp Modin
Belgrade, ME
1983

Then there were the Friday night Shabbat dinners, when songbooks were passed out and David would preside over a sing-along. More often than not these affairs were the usual medley of '70s feel-goodery ("Leaving on a Jet Plane," "House of the Rising Sun," etc.). But sometimes, if we were lucky, David would launch into a startlingly dead-on Topolesque version of "If I Were a Rich Man." He saw himself as a modern Tevyeh, a good, poor man struggling to keep the faith in a rapidly changing world. And when he sang, he would let himself go, his muscular arms swaying overhead like some ecstatic tzaddik from the Pale of Settlement, straining to touch God. And we young men would all watch with rapt attention as the image of this beautiful giant etched itself into our impressionable Tabula Judaica.

And this is what we thought:

Here is a man who knows how to live.

Here is a Jew who has found the secret to balancing the secular and sublime.

Here is a man.

Apocrypha emanated from David like spores from a dandelion. The stories were legion, yet all seemed to follow a similar thread. He had served in the Mossad. He had once killed an Egyptian with his bare hands. Every year after the campers left, one story went, David turned the camp into an antiterrorist training facility for Israeli agents. Outrageous as these stories were, we campers understood implicitly that they were not to be questioned, but rather, they were to be savored, like a good campfire ghost story.

I have one David Adler story I absolutely know to be true. I know it because I was there. It happened the summer of 1986, my first year as a junior counselor. One afternoon I was in charge of driving the shuttle van back and forth from the boys' side to the girls' side. I got an urgent call to drive to David's house immediately. The details were sketchy, but apparently something had happened at the girls' waterfront. As I pulled up to David's lakefront house, the door opened and out he came, 9 mm pistol in hand.

"Drive," he said, affectless, closing the van door.

I slammed on the gas, and off we sped to the girls' side while David inserted bullets slowly and methodically into an empty cartridge.

I asked him what was happening. He did not respond.

Finally, as if snapping out of some fugue state, he said, "Some drunk hicks swam up onto the girls' side beach. Now they're walking through the girls' side causing trouble."

To explain—at the time, my camp was situated on a beautiful lake deep in the heart of central Maine, on the outskirts of a town called Canaan (even the name reinforced our feeling of biblical destiny). The people of the town, who liked to be called Canaanites but whom we called "hicks," were a hardscrabble lot, with an angry intensity not usually found in their Southern white trash cousins. Like our Israeli brethren and their Palestinian counterparts, we campers had to share our sacred Lake George with these sullen townies, who loved nothing more than to kick back on the shore, drinking beers and smoking weed. It was a tenuous peace we held, but a peace it was. Occasionally, a group of hicks would get drunk and hassle some campers driving into town. But nothing really horrible ever happened. At least not until that fateful day.

I took my eyes off the road to watch Dave slam the cartridge into the magazine. Racking the slide, he turned to me and offered the slightest of grins.

"Mark VII Desert Eagle. Israeli-made. Finest handgun in the world."

Instantly, the sweat began cascading down my back, straight into my quivering, cosseted, upper-middle-class ass crack. What the hell am I doing, I thought. I should be out showing my campers the finer points of Frisbee golf, not driving this madman to some psychotic summer-camp appointment with death.

Time for such thoughts rapidly vanished as we pulled onto the access road to the girls' side. Immediately, we saw them. Three whippet-thin youths in their late teens, gamboling down the road in frayed, holey jean shorts, shirtless, laughing. I looked over. David's eyes had gone dead. Calmly, too calmly, he told me to pull over.

I complied.

David hopped out, Desert Eagle in hand, and started walking toward the young gentlemen. From the van, I watched the boys catch sight of this strange, hulking man and his gun, watched as their faces took on expressions of intense concern. I remember desperately wanting to know what David's face looked like to them. I watched as David lifted up the gun and pointed it at them.

"You boys heading for the road?" he asked.

"Yes sir," they answered, their terror palpable.

"Excellent. Just to be clear, you set foot on my camp one more time and I'll take this gun and blow holes in your chests. B'seder?"

These young men didn't know what *b'seder* meant, but they knew what he meant, and that was all that mattered.

"Relax, man, we're leaving! We're goin' right now!"

And so we escorted the wayward youths to the highway, where they promptly fled for safer havens. Job done, David hopped in the van and off we went.

That was it. End of confrontation.

In the end, David didn't lose his temper. He didn't shoot the kids. All he did was overreact like the coolest, most Semitic Steve McQueen I had ever seen. As I sat there in that van quaking with excitement and awe, I intuitively grasped what my ancestors knew lo those many millennia ago, that the terms *badass* and *Jew* are not by definition oxymoronic. Witnessing my camp director in action that sublime summer's day, I experienced the same adrenaline rush those wandering Semites must have felt when they encircled Jericho with Joshua, the same buzz those intrepid Zionists must have had riding into Lydda with Dayan back in '48. Let the goyim have their John Wayne, I thought to myself.

I have David Adler. Camp director.

Stuart Blumberg
(second from left)
Camp Modin, Belgrade, ME
1980

Rock Lobster

"Everybody's rockin'
Everybody's fruggin'"
—The B-52's

The critical aspect of mealtimes was that they were one of the few times the entire camp was under one roof. This was the time when gossip could ripple through the camp like a good Klingon joke at a Star Trek convention.

From a gastronomic perspective, breakfast was often the main event. Campers would jockey for position at the cereal bar, devouring bowls of the sugared brands they were forbidden to consume at home like hyenas stripping the carcass of a hapless wildebeest. Aside from the excitement of the items served on special days—Grilled Cheese Tuesday, Ice Cream Sunday, Fried Chicken Fridays—the foodstuffs served only seemed to exist in camp, as if it was a parallel universe. FrozFruit pops, Vienna Fingers, and the Ritz cracker knockoffs, Bitz Crackers, just did not crop up with any regularity back in the real world. To make it through the summer, campers were forced to rely on the supplies they stashed, often illegally, back at the bunk—Pillsbury cookie dough consumed straight from the tube, a family bag of Cool Ranch Doritos, or half a Big Mac carefully stored away since the last day trip, all washed down with a warm can of orange soda.

Luckily, food was often the last thing on your mind at mealtime. The dining room was awash with the spontaneous singing of ritualized bunk songs, renditions of current smash hits and even some original compositions, which, though they appeared nonsensical, often gained instant popularity. Every song had a purpose. If you understood them in the same way an ornithologist can recognize the calls of communal garden birds, you could learn which of the older campers wanted the counselors to notice them or who had a crush on whom and what they were going to do about it, making mealtimes the camp equivalent of *The MacNeil/Lehrer NewsHour*.

Alan Bowes
Camp Sequoia
Rock Hill, NY
1989

FRENCH WOODS
JULY 1979
ANIMAL HOUSE

Kitchen help was sectioned off at the top of the hill,
away from the rest of the camp.

Doug Grad, French Woods, Hancock, NY
1979

Our head chef was Jean. Twice a summer, to thank him, he would be routed from the kitchen by us all chanting his name until he came out. This would trigger the chant of "Speech! Speech! Speech!" and before he had the chance to open his mouth, we would cheer and drown out his words.

Mark Lamster, Camp Tomahawk, Bristol, NH

Camp Tamakwa
Algonquin Park,
ON, Canada
1979

The still lifes are really hard to put my finger on. I think I took them as a way to remember the minutiae of camp and the atmosphere it evoked, not just the people and the activities. This is breakfast. I was on kitchen duty that day and I had to set the tables . . . so I took a picture of my handiwork.

David Measer
Bar 717 Ranch Camp, Trinity, CA
c. 1980

No Friday night at camp was complete without enjoying Frieda's special fried chicken dinner, complete with mashed potatoes, green peas, and baked rolls. You could smell across camp the masses of chicken frying beginning as early as 3:30 in the afternoon. The fried chicken was eventually phased out to every other week, presumably for health-related reasons. We would ritually bang on the table and shout the "Frieda Song" in homage to her.

Eric Michaels, Camp Walden, Cheboygan, MI
1990

Jacobs Camp
Utica, MS
c. 1980

Julie Jacobs
Camp Lochearn
Post Mills, VT
1983

Camp was all about Cool Ranch Doritos (never nachos), Pringles, and anything with sugar. We would would consume Kool-Aid powder right from the packet or iced-tea mix straight out of the can, even though I once spilled Kool-Aid powder on a kid's bed and it burned right through the mattress.

Jackie Kristel, Camp Merriwood, Orford, NH

We had a diet table that you put yourself on. You pretty much just ate fruit and got weighed every week. If dessert was good, the whole room would shout, *"Hey diet table—Whoopie Pies!"*

Deb Bander, Camp Matoaka, Oakland, ME

We would smoke dried rose petals out of a Coke can and pretend to get high. We would lie there talking about boys and about the other girls.

Sloane Crosley, Camp Wa-klo, Keane, NH

A counselor and a counselor in training in the wake of a huge food fight during the all-camp barbecue.

Rachel Cohen, Camp Judaea, Hendersonville, NC
1987

I knew exactly what I was doing when the food began to fly. Just like in a pool hall, where the people in the know grab the balls to fight and leave the novices to grab the sticks, I knew exactly how to cause maximum damage by throwing the tray while making it look like another table should be blamed. However, punishments were widespread and instant. I spent much of my summer in chain gang–like conditions setting rat traps by the garbage skips.

David Light, Camp Ramah in the Poconos, Lake Como, PA

Main Street Variety Pizza. The counselors ran a scam where they would charge us $25 to bring back a pizza. Then we realized we could short-circuit the system by having the store deliver. We would creep out of our bunks and meet them behind the Rec Hall.

Nick Kroll, Camp Wildwood, Bridgton, ME

CAMP METABOLISM

BY RODNEY ROTHMAN

There were no locks on the bathroom stall doors at Camp Lindenmere. So naturally I became paranoid that when I went to the bathroom another camper, not realizing I was there, would burst into the unlocked stall. So I resolved never to go to the bathroom for the entire four-week period that I was at camp.

Making it to the two-day point was easy, even for a suburban ten-year-old accustomed to easy living and immediate gratification. In fact I barely thought about going to the bathroom at all. In the early days of summer camp, campers establish the pecking order for the entire summer. You learn who's good at hockey, who already uses deodorant, who tells the most believable lies about having touched a girl. It's a tense, stressful period that lends itself to a rigid bowel.

By the third day of camp, I felt confident I was not the biggest loser in the bunk. I was firmly in the middle of the pack, gloriously unexceptional, an authority on nothing, a companion to many. On the third night, after lights-out, we stayed up until midnight telling ghost stories. Years before, the summer camp had been the site of a ghastly series of murders, committed by a twelve-year-old boy with a lacrosse stick. It sounded implausible but was absolutely true. He had run off into the woods, and was likely still alive, living off roots and leaves in the winter, and feasting on our fruit punch and leftover pans of lasagna in the summer. The story was terrifying, but I felt safe tucked inside my bed, perfectly located in the middle of the room, far away from the screen doors and windows that would be sliced open by his razor-sharp lacrosse stick.

By the fourth day I was in great physical pain. Mainly due to stomach cramps and an acute pinching of the upper sphincter. Three days of chicken strips and steak fingers, as well as Mexican Night, had formed a bloat of desiccated waste matter in my colon. Plainly put, I really needed to go to the bathroom. I tried not to sleep on my stomach or tie the strings on my bathing suit too tightly. And when we played intramural basketball, forget about running.

On the fifth night we gathered in the rec room and watched *Night of the Living Dead* projected onto a portable movie screen. Each time a zombie jumped from the darkness my stomach would tighten and a tiny piece of feces would force its way through my lower sphincter and into my anal canal, poking its dazed head out into my shorts for a moment, before my body angrily retracted it into my rectum. At the end of the film our hero, Ben, having outlasted the zombie horde for ninety minutes, emerges safely from the basement into the morning light, only to be mistaken for a zombie and shot dead by an overzealous posse member. I longed for the release that Ben felt, the peace that must have passed through him when he realized he did not have to fight anymore.

Rodney Rothman
Camp Lindenmere
Henryville, PA
1986

On the seventh day my bowels and sphincter had settled into an eerie, Zen-like quiet. It appeared that the worst might be over. During morning cleanup, my bunk mate Glen told me a dirty joke about a dead farm girl who fornicated so much semen poured out of her ears. The concept shocked me. What if my bowels' pause might just be a brief moment before my head was forcefully ripped from my neck by a fecal geyser? And what was I so afraid of, anyway? That one of my bunk mates, my new friends, would accidentally enter the bathroom stall while I was in there? Would it really be so bad for them to see me hunched over on the toilet, my privates safely hidden beneath the hem of my T-shirt? Especially in our wake of our bond-strengthening sixth-day prank, in which we had stolen our counselor's plastic Mr. Spock doll, which had been given to him by his dead mother, and hung it from the rafters in an apparent toy suicide. There was a condom wrapped around Spock's doll face like a tiny latex torture hood. That project had really brought all us kids together.

I sat on the toilet seat, cold, and waited for the movement to come.

I noticed the flaked blue paint on the inside of the stall door; the holes where the lock bolts used to sit, now filled with a residual film of rust. Ten minutes passed with no sign of relief. I wasn't worried. It was still an hour

173

before lunchtime, and some part of me was wallowing in the melancholy of a sad good-bye and wanted the moment prolonged. Years later, I read that John Wayne died with over forty pounds of impacted feces in his body. It was attributed to his gruffness and willpower, but I understood the Duke's secret: why he couldn't bear to part with the stuff that had kept him company for so long, like a trusty, loyal dog that lives inside your body.

I didn't hear anyone enter the bathroom while I waited to move my bowels. I didn't realize anyone was there at all until the door of my stall was vigorously kicked open. Then the masked figure was upon me, maniacally waving a lacrosse stick while squeezing out a loud, strangled cry that echoed off the canted wooden roof. I instinctively screamed and withdrew into a fetal position. I felt the chill of cold air on my exposed balls as the ghost child began to beat the lacrosse stick loudly on the stall walls. Then the ghost child laughed, pulled his hockey mask off. The ghost child was in fact not a ghost. He was Darren from Port Jefferson, who had arrived at camp with at least five different sweater vests. Darren laughed harder, motioning my entire bunk in from the bedroom to stare at me. With the stall door wide open, I felt the first piece of shit pass my anus and fall into the bowl.

Jacobs Camp, Utica, MS
c. 1980

Mealtimes were as much about singing as they were about food. We had "dedications," camp shout-outs where the whole table would deliver a message. If someone was rumored to have given someone a handjob in a back room at a social, the whole table would scream, *"This is dedicated to Lauren. . . . You did a great job. Come in the back room and clean it up."*

Rachel Kane, Camp Che-Na-Wah, Minerva, NY

Our no-hands pudding-eating competitions were the stuff of legend. Kids went mental disposing of the stuff. One kid got his bowl and just poured it down his own pants. I got dressed down by Al Jaworski, the seventy- year-old swim instructor who was my nemesis, for "letting a child rub pudding on his dick and on his ass."

Andrew Goldberg, Camp Wildwood, Bridgton, ME

SOCIALS

Safety Dance

"We can dance, we can dance,
Everybody's takin' the chance"
—Men Without Hats

"All dressed up and nowhere to go" took on new meaning in the social, summer camp's equivalent of prison's conjugal visit. The anticipation was electric—especially at the all-girls camps, where the arrival of the opposite sex on a school bus from a neighboring camp was greeted by an outbreak of uncontainable enthusiasm matched only by Tattoo watching the plane land at the beginning of *Fantasy Island*. All of this took place after hours of outfit changes and arguments in the girls' bunk over who could borrow whose EG's and Temp a Temp. A thick mist of Drakkar Noir and Fahrenheit aftershave hung over the boys' side as cologne and deodorant had been sprayed near every part that moved.

The race often got off to a slow start. The two sexes would come together to the sounds of Blondie, Violent Femmes, or Frankie Goes to Hollywood. Although the more forward would meet *Hart to Hart*–style, with a passion that knew no bounds, the majority stood around and watched, straining to give off an air of nonchalant cool but barely able to mask the mix of terror and confusion that gripped them. An epic rock ballad could be counted on to warm things up. After that, the evening became a race to the prime makeout places—behind the stage, in the janitor's closet, at the canoe house—which, with their differing levels of privacy, would determine the base you could ultimately get to. At the end of the night, the counselors would come out with a big flashlight to tear campers apart. There was always, guaranteed, one girl missing. While the counselors mounted a search, back at the bunk the campers would lie in their beds, share munchies, and talk breathlessly about the passionate love action that had just gone down.

Gillian Laub
Trail's End Camp
Beach Lake, PA
1988

177

Every Saturday night was the camp social, held in the field house. We'd put on our tightest Cavaricci jeans and coolest Cosby sweaters, mousse up our hair, and slather ourselves in Drakkar. It was never sprayed directly *onto* the skin. You had to mist the air and walk on through. Who knew what the magical night would have in store? A slow dance to Richard Marx? A dramatic breakup? Or perhaps our golden goal—a slobbery makeout session with some under-the-shirt over-the-bra action—or the Holy Grail: sloppy second. And then Jerry, our bunk bully, topped us all. Much to our dismay, he was the first guy in our cabin to get to third base. It was hard to believe that a proper young woman would even touch such a raging asshole. On our walk home, he made us gather around and sniff his fingers. We did.

Adam Goldberg, Camp Echo Lark, Poyntelle, PA
1987

You would dig out your one pair of nice jeans. Tuck in your coolest T-shirt. Brush your hair for the first time in weeks. The whole bunk of boys would look like polished turds exchanging false bravado as we took turns standing in front of the mirror. "Dude, I am totally hooking up tonight." We were trying to build our own confidence. But we knew we were in for a miserable night. Nobody danced. None of us knew how to even talk around girls. All right—one or two of us were awesome dancers and could do the running man or could pull that move where you hold your leg and kind of jump through it. Those guys were pussy magnets. Socials were all about killing time until the last twenty minutes when everything changed and it became a mad scramble to get a slow dance. This would transition into "taking a walk" and making out or at least getting a peck on the cheek. Anything that would allow you to go back to the bunk and talk boldly about how she "really wanted you," before we went to bed and listened in the dark to the counselors exchanging tall stories: "Yes, she sucked my dick like a lollipop." Or, "I ate her out like a jar of Jell-O." None of which were remotely true.

Andrew Goldberg, Camp Wildwood, Bridgton, ME

8/80

Skylake Yosemite Camp
P. O. Box 25
Wishon, California 93669

Dear dad and mom,

How are you? I'm fine. Yesterday we had the Olympics. I didn't win anything. Last night I danced the slow dance with a girl (Kim) and she was taller that me. It was a long dance (Stairway to Hevan). A Junior staff member tryed to cut in but I didn't let him. She laught (Him) and told all of her friends. She was so taller then me, (about 5½ inches) by the end of the dance, me neck ached. Today our counsler is Jamie Otis (Steve knows him). He's our counsler because Dave went to S. F. to see the Giants play baseball

Love,

David.

P.S.- Thanks For the Care package!
P.P.S. - Save the newsletter enclosed

David Katznelson
Skylake Yosemite Camp
Wishon, CA
1980

Every girls' camp had its own vibe and reputation. Some were prissy; others had Hooter girls. Belvoir Terrace was the one we looked forward to with anticipation. We were either home or away like a sporting match. The primping was such a big deal. It could consume the whole day. We would take a bunch of showers and then slap on anything that smelled good. Mennen Speed Stick—the green one—was de rigueur. I had never heard of deodorant before I came to camp. We would roll it on all over our body. The final step was the Old Spice, which we doused ourselves in before leaving the bunk, even though most of us were not even close to shaving.

Scott Jacoby, Camp Greylock, Becket, MA

The whole summer was trial and error—a massive sexual experiment—a safe and open environment, where the girls did not run the risk of being labeled a slut forever as they did in high school. Plus, everyone socialized on the same schedule. You would come back and compare notes and hear from your bunk mates about what they got up to and with whom. And that would put ideas into your head that you were determined to try at the next social. And you could bank on the fact that the girl would go back and tell her bunk and get them up to speed on the new maneuver. We would talk to the guy about the act itself—whatever base it was—and hear about the technique in exquisite detail, giving him an opportunity to talk about new techniques of French kissing that we clung onto with rapt attention.

Mark Boxer
Camp Watitoh, Becket, MA

Lauren Senderoff
Camp Echo Lark
Poyntelle, PA
1989

In 1978, the DJs played "Copacabana" at every dance. We thought it was the greatest song. "I Will Survive" dominated 1979. "Rock Lobster," 1980. It was easy to understand why we thought the Quiana shirts were so fresh. One hundred percent polyester never looked so good. Our dances were amazing. For one thing, we had a slew of nerdy tech guys working the lights and soundboards and changing the records. For another, we were always with girls, so that left the emphasis on the dance. And we had people who were straight out of the *Fame* movie making their moves.

Doug Grad, French Woods, Hancock, NY
1978

Sari Sharaby
Camp Eisner, Great Barrington, MA
1992

Bunk S dressed up in tie-dye and Keds for a coed social. In the early '90s it was well known that bright colors were an aphrodisiac to the pubescent male. Lots of time had been spent on the hair, ensuring the bangs had enough but not too much poof as this was no longer the '80s.

Erika Vogel, Camp Saginaw, Oxford, PA
1991

gorgeous! we held hands all day' & I didn't even have a nervous stomache! I'm growing-up. I think I'm in love! I cant stop thinking about him. Thank you so much for the books! they're great!

I love you,

Katie

Katie Rosman
Camp Thunderbird
Bemidji, MI
1986

THE SOCIAL

BY JAMIE DENBO

My whole bunk, pre-social. I am sporting a hot pink Esprit—the Prada of 1980s camp fashion. In the back row. We all got the memo about white flats. Phew!

So many men, so little time. This is the sentiment that would go through my head as I applied one last layer of Revlon's Pink Foil lipstick or gave my deeply Sun-In-damaged locks one more spritz of Aqua Net. The social. That twice-monthly event that brought boys and girls together. Literally together. Her iron grip clamped down on his shoulders; his sweaty fingers delicately lying over her hips.

The bimonthly Saturday-evening social stood alone as a true oddity at camp simply because at the social you were encouraged to flirt with and even touch members of the opposite sex, while at every other camp event this kind of behavior was verboten. I knew a girl who got caught making out with a boy on a day trip in the house of mirrors at Canobie Lake Park in New Hampshire. She was sent home. That was apparently a way worse crime than getting caught eating nonkosher on a trip day, which got Joy Loeb only a stern warning that same summer.

The beautification process for a camp social was akin to that of a junior prom, except that we were younger than prom age by more than a few years and we treated it with far more importance. Camp is also where so many of the tools you would need for the rest of your lady life were discovered, and by prom time, most of these practices were already well established. Camp was where I first shaved my legs (I attended more than one social covered in glittery Band-Aids from knee to ankle), applied mascara (our whole bunk braved conjunctivitis as we applied Stacey Fink's one battered bottle of electric-blue paste), used a tampon (thank you to the Skolnick twins, who talked me through it from the other side of the toilet stall), and wore deodorant, perfume, and body spray (all at the same time).

And then, of course, there was the problem of what to wear. For prom, you shop for days. At camp, you shop for hours—in everyone else's trunks. Getting an outfit together was a scientific process that involved mixing, matching, and most important, borrowing. "I'll lend you my white denim Guess mini if you lend me your beaded and fringed Camp Beverly Hills crop top." It was imperative that your pinks didn't clash and your labels were up to par, because in our little lady brains we were absolutely positive

the boys would notice. Boys dominated presocial conversation as we flitted around, borrowing curling irons and debating the pink rhinestone bracelet versus the rainbow bead one. "I think Ross Weiner is cuter than Aaron Shore, but Ross likes Marci Glickstein so it doesn't even matter!" And so on and so on.

The other significant difference between prom and social was that at prom there is only one guy per girl. Here, there were whole bunks full of possibilities. Before us were several dozen potential suitors with whom to dance, each awash in their older brother's Ralph Lauren or Drakkar Noir, each dressed in crisp polos sent by overbearing mothers just for occasions like the social or the Color War banquet, each sporting a "wet look" with a touch too much Dippity-Do, and each desperately self-conscious about whatever acne breakout, voice-deepening crack, or other cruel trick of adolescence had decided to rear up for this once-every-two-weeks happening.

I was all poise and confidence when I stepped out of the bunk with the other girls, each of us in one Esprit ensemble or another. I bragged along with the others about just how many mediocre players of the Camp Tel Noar softball team I would enchant by evening's end. But by the time we arrived at the freshly crepe-papered doorway to the rec hall, my swagger had morphed into something more like abject fear.

At camp, there was flirting, eye-lowering, giggling, and snickering all day every day, but at the social, there was no pretense. There was action. There was no hiding from the fact that if you "liked" that person, you had to prove

What can I say about this shot except—HAIR HAIR HAIR. I think, except for when we were sleeping, this was what we focused on most while in the bunk.

**Jamie Denbo
Camp Tel Noar
Hampstead, NH
1986**

your like in front of people by publicly wrapping bony wrists around the correct anatomical locale. And you would face each other, blushing in a blotchy, rather than romantic, way, making awkward small talk about volleyball or the upcoming production of a pared-down *Guys and Dolls* during "Stairway to Heaven." And you would never know how to dance during the fast part. And when the last croaky line, ". . . and she's buy-uy-ing a stairway . . . to Heav-e-en," finally ends your nine minutes and forty-nine seconds of torture, elation, nausea, and ecstasy, your bunk will get called together, and you will be marched off to bed. And you will endure endless teasing about how on earth you could possibly like Marcus Fagell more than Howie Deutchman. And you will realize you lost your favorite gummy bracelet somewhere on the dance floor. And you will cry because you loved that gummy. But the best part about the lost gummy is that by the time you have settled into your bottom bunk and Debbie Weinstein has soothed you by promising to give you her extra gummy that she never wears anyway, everyone will have forgotten about the public slow dancing with Marcus. And as you fall asleep, you can think about what you will be wearing when he is delicately holding your hips at the next social in two weeks.

We were getting ready for a social with our brother camp, Greylock. Unbeknownst to each other, we both had decided to go with the Debbie Gibson look, hat and all. Before every social, we paraded our outfits around the camp for hours before making our debut with the boys. This picture was taken right outside of the oldest girls' bunk, who gave us the ultimate thumbs-up on these winning ensembles. The boys were after us all night.

Lori Harrison, Camp Romaca, Hinsdale, MA
1989

Kate Lee
Camp Eisner
Great Barrington, MA
1991

At our all-girls camp we lived for the socials because we were allowed to dress out of uniform and something other than navy and white polyester. Our dance did not involve boys across the lake. It was literally just a DJ with all the Tega girls dressed out of uniform.

Sara Solfanelli, Camp Tegawitha, Tobyhanna, PA

At the end of the night, we would walk back from the rec hall to return to our units. Girls to the left. Boys to the right. We were given three seconds to kiss good night. The counselors would stand there and time you.

Lauren Stein, Camp Pinemere, Stroudsburg, PA

The first love of my life was Pablo Cohen, aka Paul. We met at Maine Teen Camp in Kezar Falls, Maine, the summer I was fourteen. He was from Rio Piedras, a suburb of San Juan, Puerto Rico. He was tan and sweet and because I was about to start in Spanish II in high school, I thought he was a great choice for my summer boyfriend. I can't help but still have his good-bye message to me memorized: "Dear Rebecca, I had the best summer of my life with you. I will miss you. You have the most beautiful eyes in the whole world. Love, Paul. PS. Remember—I will always love you."

It was the last night of the summer. Several of my friends (none of the ones in the picture above, to be clear!) were sluts. There was immense social pressure to catch up. I had to come back having given a handjob. Socials were well-orchestrated affairs. We'd dance to New Order's "Bizarre Love Triangle" and then we'd quickly disperse to the woods for a five-minute makeout session before we were forced to retreat to our bunks for the night. I remember the last night, it was 10:00 p.m. and the first whistle blew to mark the winding down of the evening. It was now or never. I had to do it. I was petrified. I stuck my hands down his pants and found a tiny little soft thing. I grasped it—was struck by how small it was and how wet it felt. I snapped my hand back out. And that was it. I went home so proud. I was now officially a slut.

Rebecca Shapiro (second from right)
Camp Walden, Cheboygan, MI
1990

190

you're gunna flip – but I'm not
a slut (where I live at least)

The weekly socials at camp gave me a taste of what it must have felt like for the Beatles when they first came to America. There was screaming, tears, and then lots of underage rumpy pumpy. My English accent went over really well. The girls were like flies on shit.

Michael Cohen
Camp Louemma, Sussex, NJ
1991

Making Love Out of Nothing at All

> "I know when to pull you closer
> And I know when to let you loose"
> —Air Supply

Camp was many things: the place you learned to swim, played Nathan Detroit onstage to middling reviews, or shaved your legs for the first time. But above all, it was a sizzling petri dish of sexual exploration. This is the equation: a massive peer group + teen supervision + being in the great outdoors with little else to do at night + a thousand secret hiding places + those new feelings you're experiencing in your pants = makeout city. There was no better place to master the sensual art of swapping saliva than at camp, where you could grind away until curfew and then have your whole bunk waiting to analyze your technique like a NASCAR pit crew.

This was true for heterosexuals as well as homosexuals, who, turned on by experimenting with cross-dressing thanks to the theater department, also had the opportunity to practice their moves. Even if you never got any action at all in high school, you could still get something at camp, because this was a place where your real-life experience could be hidden, offering boys a chance to start over and cast themselves anew as ladies' men. For the girls, camp was a progenitor of "What Happens in Vegas, Stays in Vegas," a place where you could get up to just about anything without staining your carefully cultivated hometown reputation. As a result, most campers' strategy was to gun for quantity over quality. Any relationship over two days was a long-term commitment, and life was lived on a roller coaster of intense emotion in which the time span between the thrill of a crush, the pleasure of a kiss, and the shattering despondency of a breakup matched the life cycle of a mayfly.

Jenna Fallon
Camp Edward Isaacs
Holmes, NY
1988

193

This was a sweet time in life when we were so young. Brad and I dated for a little more than two years, at summer camp and at home as well. Dating consisted of listening to a lot of Led Zeppelin and Pink Floyd, spending days and nights sitting at the beach, and having his arm around me like this, pretty much all of the time.

Barbi Stalburg Bell
Camp Walden
Cheboygan, MI
1988

I fell for Ricky Epstein my last summer at Camp Watitoh. He drove the waterski boat. We dated for the first half of the summer and then I broke up with him for no reason other than I thought I was ignoring my best friend Lauren and that it was hurting our friendship. Ricky got back at me by dating another girl in my bunk. I then had to suffer through many nights of listening to them fool around just three cots away from me when he visited her on late-night raids.

Amy Israel
Camp Watitoh
Becket, MA
c. 1986

Pat Byrne. Undoubtedly the cutest boy at camp and a great letter writer for a twelve-year-old. His highest act of devotion was that he wrote out by hand the lyrics to "American Pie" for me. We had a "love affair" over two summers. It definitely hurt that I grew four inches between summers. On the last day of camp we were both hysterically crying even though we only lived about twenty-five minutes apart in New Jersey. We both knew it was unlikely we would stay together.

Melissa Brown Eisenberg
Hidden Valley Camp, Freedom, ME
1990

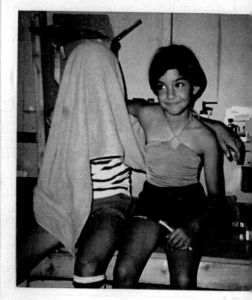

The boy on the left is my boyfriend, Eric Sherman. The boy in the right Polaroid is another boy with a towel on his head—a stand-in to make Eric Sherman jealous.

Deborah Gitell, Camp Kingswood, Bridgton, ME
1983

I was a sexual being at camp who did things I would never do at home in high school. I went out with a guy called Mike who was three years older, which was way older when you were fourteen. He was hot to me because everyone said he was hot. We ended up in the makeout spot by the hip-hop classroom and hooked up. I was in the middle of giving him a handjob when he said "not quite" and left me there on my own, devastated. I went back to the bunk and told my best friend, the popular Natasha. I woke up in the morning feeling as if my life was over. Natasha burst in laughing. I was like, What happened? She said she went out and met Mike. Went down to the waterfront. Told him to take off his shirt. So he took off his shirt. Told him to take off his pants. So he did. Boxers. Did. "And now I am not going to do anything to you." And left him standing there on his own, naked. That is a camp friendship right there. And that is camp in a nutshell. One minute you feel like your life is over, the next you feel all-powerful. And your mom never hears about anything.

Ariel Relbrooke, Camp Echo Lark, Poyntelle, PA

I developed a patented money move guaranteed to get you to second base. "The back-to-front back rub" starts off as a friendly, innocent back rub. Then you slowly start to move into a reach-around. From nonthreatening massage to salacious lover. This works all the way up to college.

David Light, Camp Ramah in the Poconos, Lake Como, PA

Seventh grade. I convinced the girls' bunk to do an early-stage breast cancer screening. We were all going into eighth grade. We had hormones that were out of control. I blurted out they all needed to get ready for me to feel them up and screen them. Voluptuous or flat, they were all amenable.

Alex Grossman, Camp Tamarack, Ortonville, MI

I was caught fooling around with my boyfriend during a nighttime screening of Big Business. My punishment was to miss a dance and to call my parents. My life felt like it was so over. My parents didn't say much when I called, but when they came up to Visiting Day, they gave me the "your body is your temple" speech. When I was caught fooling around, I had to tell the camp director details. He wrote it all down. He wanted to know what I did. What I said. Where I touched. You are so scared and you love camp so much, you tell him everything. They have acres of information—East German secret police quantities—on each camper, kept on index cards. How we slept. Our appetites. Bowel movements. Our teeth.

Lauren Stein, Camp Pinemere, Stroudsburg, PA

Stacy Horne
Camp Nah-Jee-Wah
Milford, PA
1989

"Why I love...

Jeff

If the sun refused to shine
I would still be loving you
When mountains crumble to-
and me
There will still be you

THANK - LED
YOU ZEP

YOU'LL BE HAPP

Okay, maybe it won't turn in
great love of your life. But bo
be happy while it lasts, and t
matters most. The trick is keepin
romances in perspective: By c
they're not built to last forever. J
them for the short-lived but ultr
experiences that they are. Sort of
cola of relationships.

-ZOG-

5 PTS.
BETWEEN
SHIFTS

Can you make it
to your next
PayDay?

ATTN: ALL MAIL MEN W/ HOT BODIE-
SIGN Here:

X _____ —
X _____
X _____
X _____ ᵇ˙
X _____
X _____
X _____
X _____

Lindsay Weiss
Camp Vega, Kent Hills, ME
1991

Singing on the beach.
This was a day off in
Charlevoix, in 1985, our
first year as counselors.
We would sing and get
w-a-a-a-y tan.

Liz Stevens
Camp Walden
Cheboygan, MI
1985

SUMMER ROMANC

I fell in love with a counselor when I was twelve. He was my first real love. We would sit on the dock at night, telling each other secrets all night. Or I would sit on the piano bench while he played "Desperado." He had a Mohawk. He was an outsider. People thought he was arrogant and that he was a bullshitter, but I believed all his stories. This relationship was so profound for me. I got him in a way no one else did. I understood him. He told me he would come and find me when he was eighteen. I always believed him. He never did.

Lauren Sandler, Camp Wyonegonic, Denmark, ME

The big deal at my camp was when you kissed a boy at the Camp Deerfield social. You would ask him for his sweatshirt to prove it, and in the morning after a social, loads of girls would show up for breakfast wearing a big D sweatshirt to show you had got yours. This was a badge of honor, but the reality was that in most cases we would kiss quickly and then demand a sweatshirt. What did I learn about men from camp? That they are pawns. Something to obsess about at the time. I can't remember any of their names now. They really only brought happiness if you had a bunk full of girlfriends to discuss them with. If you made out with someone and you never got to share and discuss it, what's the point? Hence the Deerfield sweatshirt.

Jackie Kristel, Camp Merriwood, Orford, NH

The thing I valued about going to an all-girls camp was having the opportunity to develop a social life and friendships with girls based on how you really related to each other, as opposed to just revolving around boys. Camp was two months a year when boy relationships were not significant at all, other than the phantom camp boyfriends we saw at the two camp socials a summer and wrote letters of flirtation to. When we did see them, we were far too embarrassed to kiss them in person. I always had a platonic boyfriend every summer. We never kissed.

Katie Rosman, Camp Thunderbird, Bemidji, MN

Camp got better once I learned to hook up. A week was a long relationship. I was a quantity man until the last summer. There was a group of popular kids—a clique of six boys and six girls who all dated each other and rotated partners during the summer. That left the rest of us. AIDS was a topic of constant conversation. It was a menace. In our minds, we all wanted to sleep with girls, but if one wanted to sleep with you, it meant she had slept with other people, which meant that she most probably had AIDS. At the same time, this was a community—and it should have felt safe to be promiscuous. But the world outside was so fixated with AIDS that we were all terrified.

Mik Moore, Camp Tel Yehudah, Barryville, NY

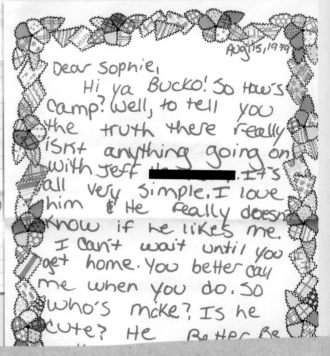

Hi How are you
do you bealive what
Mary was going to
do with him oh.
my god I niver

knew she was like
that I also found
out that she
gave him a blow
Job Holy Shit
tell you more →

Aug 15, 1979

Dear Sophie,
Hi ya BUCKO! So How's
camp? Well, to tell you
the truth there really
isn't anything going on
with Jeff ████████. It's
all very simple. I love
him & He really doesn't
know if he likes me.
I can't wait until you
get home. You better call
me when you do. So
who's make? Is he
cute? He Better Be

My first kiss was with Roger Levenson. I had practiced on a peach all afternoon in the cafeteria before the social. At lunch all of my bunk quizzed me: "Are you going to kiss Roger tonight?" They gave me a peach, cut it in half and I started to tongue it. The whole bunk shouted *"Dedication! Silence please."* (Silence.) "Dedicated to Ariel Schwartz. Ariel is practicing with the peach for Roger tonight."

Why Roger? He asked me to dance. That was sufficient to make him the One. He was a year older than me. Tall, skinny, tan, with short brown hair and thick glasses. There was a rigorous courtship ritual: Dance at the first social. Hold hands at the second. Then you just know it in your stomach after that when it is time to kiss. It is much discussed, first in the boys' camp, then word gets out and it becomes much discussed in the girls' camp. The trick is, you have to find a place to go to escape the eyes of the authorities . . . behind the bunk when the boys are escorting you off the camp. Seize the moment, head behind the bunk. I don't remember Roger saying a word to me the entire relationship. He just leaned forward and kissed me with his tongue. Then we were like "OK, bye," and I was on the ferry back across the lake to the girls' camp, the center of attention with all my friends sitting around me asking, "What was it like?" The rite of passage was done. Struck off the list. There was a great feeling of relief. You have no intention of going any further. You don't even intend to do it again.

Ariel Relbrooke, Camp Echo Lark, Poyntelle, PA

We dated for three months in eighth grade, which was a major relationship back then.

Dana Kroll, Camp Walden, Denmark, ME 1986

Dany Levy
Camp Laurel, Readfield, ME
1984

My first kiss was with Daniel S. He wrote me letters that were so intense. "I would kill for your gorgeous face." I would die to get that kind of letter now. "When we kiss I know you are for me." We were sex curious but we did not know what to do. We would sneak out in kayaks in the middle of the night, meet our boyfriends in the middle of the lake, and try and make out by floating alongside each other and just kissing.

Sloane Crosley, Camp Wa-klo, Keane, NH

Jenna Fallon
Camp Edward Isaacs, Holmes, NY
c. 1986

In the Air Tonight

"I've been waiting for this moment all my life,
Oh Lord"
—Phil Collins

Yes, the Catholics love their baptisms, the Japanese their tea ceremonies, and the Maya their bloodletting, but few cultures have woven as complex a set of rituals into the everyday as the American summer camp. The power of ritual lies in its ability to serve many functions—worship, purification, marking time, or atonement. But at camp, it plays a more practical role. Without it, two months in a bunk would seem as big and empty as the Grand Canyon, and so camp directors, with some creative brilliance, developed a litany of services, activities, and special evenings that flowed together in a known order, to give a pattern to camp life.

From camp services on Friday night or Sunday morning—campers in their finest white outfits blundering through a collection of prayers that were often customized to eliminate God and instead worship the camp itself—to the sacred events that were scattered throughout the summer, some real and some manufactured, these evenings offered campers the security of the known and the familiar. The events themselves may have been repetitive, but your role in them increased every summer, letting you inch ever nearer to the oldest campers and counselors you admired so deeply.

Camp was also packed with informal ritual. First and foremost, the evening raid, which symbolized one of the core values of camp as a place to test and break boundaries. The raid was most campers' first encounter with adrenaline. Much of the thrill lay in the elaborate preparation. Campers would lie in bed, feigning sleep until the designated hour when they would arise and don raiding garb in the dark silence of the bunk. The knot of anticipation in the pit of your stomach lasted until you had crept past the director's house, after which you were left with a sense that you, and you alone, had invented the whole concept of raiding.

A Michael Jackson lookalike came to our camp to entertain us. He was so serious he even brought his own bodyguard.

Karen Lauterstein
KenWood Camp,
Kent, CT
1983

203

Julie Jacobs
Camp Lochearn
Post Mills, VT
1982

FLAG RAISING

For flag raising, whoever got to the director's house first got to read the baseball box scores out loud. All the Mets and Yankees fans would hang on your every word. Flag lowering was the time when coaches would make reports. "Today we had a 10B hockey match against Samoset. We put up a good fight. Played a good game. Darrel Cohen got a goal and an assist. We came up short 4 to 3." I had to coach a basketball team against Cedar once and had to report in. "We put up a good fight. Lost 29 to 2. Brian Lazlow scored our basket. Neal Leon hit the backboard twice."

Andrew Goldberg, Camp Wildwood, Bridgton, ME

Flag raising at our camp was a single-sex activity. Maybe because of this, it was an exercise in indifference. You had to make it clear to everyone else you had been up all night. We would all stand there, hands in pockets, heads skyward, mouths open. We had all gone to sleep about two hours before.

David Wain, Camp Modin, Belgrade, ME

In our flagpole was soldered a copper box in which were the ashes of our camp founder. We would fight to be the one to tie the rope in sailor knots or to fold the flag in crisp military style. It was the biggest deal if you dropped the flag. I still remember the sound of a hundred girls gasping in shock if the flag hit the deck. A lot of crafty Republicana slipped into camp ritual.

Sloane Crosley, Camp Wa-klo, Keane, NH

Laser Rosenberg
Camp Modin, Belgrade, ME
c. 1983

Karen Lauterstein
KenWood Camp, Kent, CT
1988

SERVICES

On Friday night, we would all don our Shabbat white and take a special path to the dining room. The whole camp came together, ages seven to sixteen, trying to look their drop-dead best. All afternoon a battalion of Conair hair dryers had been on full blast, extra high. Makeup had been applied for the only time all week. Everything seemed like it was vaguely in soft focus, like a Linda Ronstadt album cover. And we came together as a community. Without summer camp most Jewish nerds would never have sex. All of us in our Shabbat finery in twilight, apart from the one person whose clothes had gone pink in the wash, socializing—the equivalent of dogs sniffing each other's butts. In the Shabbat ceremony, everything was mixed up. It was like a cauldron of ritual led by Fischel Kolko—an older staff member who seemed two hundred to us, like Gandalf. It was a mix of the religious and the social, but at the end of the day, we were celebrating each other and the camp at the same time.

Jack Isquith, Camp Boiberik, Rhinebeck, NY

We had a chapel where we would chant: "Service, friendship, and honesty." They would give us a candle and we would sing songs in a field, lovingly adapted from "I'd Like to Buy the World a Coke."

Ken Freimann, Camp Norwich, Huntington, MA

SPECIAL TRADITIONS

We had a camp tradition called Pie Man. You never knew when it would be. But when the camp was all together during a quiet moment, you would hear the beginning of the J. Geils Band's "Freeze Frame." And then two guys in dark glasses would come out of nowhere and hit someone—and you never knew who it would be—with a pie in the face. The people who were in on it never acknowledged it afterward and would pretend they were not involved, even though the only thing that had disguised them was a pair of dark glasses.

David Wain, Camp Modin, Belgrade, ME

Animal Farm was a tradition at our camp. You would synch with the other bunks that at 11:30 at night you would just bust out the animal noises. I was partial to the *moo*. The game would end with us all running to the flagpole and back. Totally overwhelming the night watch staff. The thrill—the feeling—as you touched the pole was so invigorating.

Jordan Roter, Tripp Lake Camp, Poland, ME

Gross-out night was when six or seven of us would get in a cabin and one would chew bread and then spit it into a bowl. The next would do the same with the lettuce, cheese, then meat. Last person in the row had to eat it.

Ken Freimann, Camp Norwich, Huntington, MA

Fourth of July carnival at camp. Every senior camp bunk ran a carnival booth and I built this Bronco Buster for mine. Not bad for a big-city boy with few arts and crafts skills. It's just an oil drum with four holes and a rope, tied among four trees.

Michael Solomon
Camp Androscoggin
Wayne, ME
1987

Pajama Day at camp, when you wore your pajamas for a day of activities, which included pillow fights, scary story competitions, and a best-pajamas contest.

Matt Dorter
Camp Poyntelle Lewis Village
Poyntelle, PA
1985

My Michael Jackson obsession was on the wane, replaced by a love affair with Morrissey and Alphaville. The Michael Jackson gloves remained handy for the "black and white" night though.

Sarah Sokolic
Camp Ramah in the
Berkshires, Wingdale, NY
1987

Our camp had an annual Fantasy Night where the older campers would dress up to create fairy-tale vignettes. Then they would wake up the smaller campers from their sleep and act out the stories, like the Candy House from "Hansel and Gretel." Then the kids were put back to bed, and in the morning none of the older campers would acknowledge the event ever took place, making it a collective head-fuck—all the kids just assumed they had the most magical dream.

Francine Hermelin, Camp Tamakwa, Algonquin Park, ON, Canada

THE RAID

Camp life really began at night. Sneaking up on the girls' camp after lights-out. At midnight, we were up and ready to sneak to the girls' side. It is hard to describe the sense of excitement of this action. Oh, the adventure! A car, headlights on full beam, triggered the cry of "car coming!" Everyone would hit the bushes. We had to walk across Route 2—the two sides of camp were over a mile apart—and then we would hang out and make out. Age twelve to thirteen, the thrill was more in the waking up and hanging out. Fourteen to fifteen, you went over with more serious intent. We felt like the coolest people in the world. Like we had invented this—the camp raid—and it was something only we knew about.

David Wain, Camp Modin, Belgrade, ME

We would dress in black like commandos for camp raids. This was my first encounter with adrenaline. The whole of camp was about breaking boundaries. Raids were the ultimate. Putting on camouflage army gear and breaking out to climb on to the roof of the director's house. Or escaping to the nearby town. Whatever I could do to break the rules and prove that there was a world outside of our camp—which always felt like the entire universe.

Scott Jacoby, Camp Greylock, Becket, MA

Our bunk would plan a raid to the boys' side for a week, as if we were storming the beaches of Normandy. All we did was try and grab a pair of underwear and get it back to our bunk.

Jenny Wiener, Camp Emerson, Hinsdale, MA

209

Missing You

> "I ain't missing you, no matter
> What my friends say"
> —John Waite

For one day every session the Neverland of camp was shattered by a sudden intrusion of reality. After both camp and campers had been thoroughly scrubbed up, the parents' arrival on Visiting Day triggered a complex set of plotlines that would play out over the couple of hours before they departed later the same afternoon.

Some campers were desperate to impress their parents with the fruits of their newfound independence, be it their slice backhand on the tennis court, their onstage thespian talents, or their lanyard-making wizardry in the arts and crafts room. Those kids who ran the camp's black market viewed the day in clinical, unemotional terms as an opportunity to organize a massive influx of Doritos, Pixy Stix, and Kool-Aid, and maintain their racket for the rest of the summer. The unfortunates who had spent the vast majority of the past five weeks sobbing with a near fatal case of homesickness treated the day as the time to execute the Great Escape—a cunning evacuation plan that would liberate them from the living hell that was camp, and return them to the loving bosom of home. This plan normally consisted of locking themselves in their parents' rental car and refusing to get out.

Whatever the angle, most parents played along, eager to assuage the guilt they felt for barely missing their children. Dumping the kids in the backwoods of nowheresville felt like a small price to pay for six luxurious weeks touring Europe. The camp staff devoted their energies single-mindedly to proving that they were treating their charges OK, so that the parents would see the fortune they were being charged as money well spent. As the first line of cars started to appear at the bottom of the camp road, camp staff waited for the drama to unfold, culminating in glory over the lobster they sprang for at dinner.

Ellen Schweber
Camp Danbee
Hinsdale, MA
1978

Visiting Day meant a parking lot packed with black cars—either Cadillac or
Mercedes. Two things stand out here: My Prince tennis racket was a major status
symbol. And my brother is wearing odd socks. We went to a uniform camp. The
only thing possible for him to get wrong he did.

Niccole Siegel, Camp Kenwood, Kent, CT
1986

The two great dinners of camp were strategically placed. One was the night before
you left for home, and one the night before Visiting Day. So when Mom asked you
what you ate for dinner last night, you would say "steak," creating the impression
that you ate that every night.

Scott Jacoby, Camp Greylock, Becket, MA

VISITING DAY

BY NICK KROLL

We spent the first half of the summer working out exactly what junk food we wanted our parents to bring up: Cheetos, orange soda, twelve-packs of Krackels, Swedish Fish. We asked for all the things we would never be allowed to eat at home but which our parents would bring up on Visiting Day to show how much they missed us. This parent booty was like the cigarettes in the jail of camp life. The night after visiting day, back at the bunk, we enacted scenes of *Caligula*-style gluttony, with orgiastic, hardcore snacking. We reclined on our bunk beds, deep in a glaze of sugar and chemicals, on the verge of blissful diarrhea, and chugged cans of lukewarm, flat orange soda for the simple fact that we could.

Two days later, our stash of goodies was rounded up on orders from the camp director. The official party line was to "protect the bunks from mice." Upon becoming counselors we learned that the bounty was moved to the head counselor's office for the counselors to pig out on. And in this way, the junk food purchased in bulk by our loving parents to demonstrate their love for us was expropriated by the camp director so he could show his love to his loyal camp staff.

The actual Visiting Day was all about the lunch buffet—the same cook responsible for "Loose Meat Tuesdays" suddenly summoned the skills to produce succulent fried chicken and fluffy yet moist cakes topped with luxurious chocolate icing. Our parents were also given the false impression that we had lemonade and iced tea in the same meal, so that if we had the whim to make an Arnold Palmer, we could do so at a moment's notice. The grandeur of this buffet was a symbol of the extent to which "Visiting Day" camp was unrecognizable compared with "rest of the summer" camp, a reality our parents were happy to ignore.

I think, perhaps, we were all too concerned with the realities of our families and the dynamics of our fellow campers' families to notice. Visiting Day was when you realized that the kid who'd been bullying everyone all summer had a dad who was just a little too tan and wore a suede safari jacket and spent all of Visiting Day ignoring his son while talking on a cell phone that required its own bag and three-foot antenna. All of sudden, it made sense why Mikey was such a little prick: his father ignored him, never spoke to his mother, and instead talked with the cute counselors from Minnesota for longer than was appropriate.

At least the kids whose parents were divorced got to make full use of the forty-eight hours of Visiting Day—one parent would come up the day after the other. Those lucky children of divorce really made out like bandits on parents' booty as Mom and Dad struggled to win their kid's love with the aid of a few extra canisters of Easy Cheese.

But parents' Visiting Day was not the only time that I shared my camp experience with the man who paid for it all. At the end of the summer, a number of fathers came up for Father/Son Weekend to get a taste of where their money had really gone. I was looking forward to this weekend all summer because I had continually boasted about how my father was a great athlete who had been drafted to play minor league baseball in Florida's Grapefruit League. It was an exciting prospect to show my friends what my father could do on the field and bask vicariously in the glow of his athleticism. I had told them he had hit such a towering home run against Don Drysdale at Dodgers Fantasy Baseball Camp that Tommy Lasorda gave him his secret lasagna recipe. So imagine my horror as I watched my dad pull up lame running to first base on a weakly hit grounder when we hit the baseball diamond early on during Father/Son Weekend. All of a sudden, I was embarrassed by this man—my father, a great jock, the founder of a multimillion-dollar business, had not delivered as advertised. It was like finding out the knives you'd ordered from a screaming Southern pitchman on QVC could not actually cut through glass, let alone a tomato.

Nick Kroll, front row, right. His father, back row, second from right. That is a cigar Andy Cohen is smoking next to me. We were ten years old. Camp Wildwood Bridgton, ME 1988

My father could sense my disgust with him being mortal as he limped quickly after me. Not one to let me down, he tried to make it up to his newly disillusioned son by taking me for a trip around the lake to prove that, while he no longer could tear up the base paths, he could still dominate the choppy waters of Lake Fake Native American Name. The conversation went something like:

"Come on, Nicky, let's go on a boat!"
"I don't want to—and you don't know how to operate a sailboat."
"Oh come on now, sport, it'll be fun. It's like driving a car, but on the water."
"But you don't drive a car. You have a driver. His name is Dominic."
"Just put on a life vest and get in the boat."

We sailed out on a little Stingray into the middle of Lake Fake Native American Name, where he decided to adjust the sail by moving his chubby, sunburned body to the other side of the boat. We capsized immediately. Both of us sat there, floating in the cold water alongside the upturned boat, staring at each other for a full two or three minutes in silence. And then I began crying with fury at my father and swam off to the shore, leaving him to deal with the boat on his own. When he returned an hour later, tired, burnt to a crisp, with an aching back, he found me in the bunk, sitting on my bed in my soaked tighty-whities. Exhausted by trying to please his fickle son, he looked at me and, for some reason, said he was sorry. I inaudibly accepted his apology. Only now do I realize that I was angry at him because he was growing older; he was no longer the young, athletic man whom I always admired. I also realize that only a real man who was confident with who he was could apologize to his son.

Since a verbal apology wasn't enough, my dad made up for his growing older by taking me out to Rick's Café, where he bought me cheeseburgers and chocolate bobblehead dolls, and topped it all off with some fine art of the cinematic variety. He took me to see *Under Siege 2* at the Mountain Valley Mall, where I witnessed a real hero who'll never grow old, one Mr. Steven Seagal.

Visiting Day was always a mixed bag. I wanted to appear strong and happy—but secretly I was wishing my folks would whisk me home. I am with my dad and my sister Jodi. I can still remember the smell of that dusty road—with the fragrant pines heating up in the summer and the wafting odors of the horse shit and human shit from the corral and the outhouses just off to the left. The Oldsmobile Vista Cruiser wagon with ski racks was my buddy Glen Bailis's folks' car.

Doug Ross, Geneva Glen Camp, Indian Hills, CO
1971

The tepees were awesome. Over the course of the summer the campers that lived there would get more and more into being part of "Indian camp" or "Indian Village" and some of them would start going barefoot and dress in native garb or with beads in their hair and stuff. A camper even wore a loincloth to a special event one night.

Melissa Brown Eisenberg
Hidden Valley Camp, Freedom, ME
1989

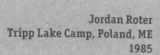

Jordan Roter
Tripp Lake Camp, Poland, ME
1985

That's me and my grandmother, Sylvia Stone, in front of the Tomahawk dining hall. I'm digging around in the bag looking for the "contraband" candy I had requested. I was a bit disappointed to find fresh plums.

Mark Lamster
Camp Tomahawk, Bristol, NH
1980

We had several naked-women pictures at camp, most of which were of Heather Locklear. This was pre–*Melrose Place* days! I actually do remember putting them up, always on the first day when we were all so excited just to be back at camp. The same kid brought the posters up. His mom sent *Playboys* throughout the summer.

Alan Bowes, Camp Sequoia, Rock Hill, NY
1989

This photo is all about parental guilt. For Visiting Day every year, my mom and dad would show up with bags full of food and presents as if camp were some sort of prison. My sister and I are eating and opening some of our gifts on my bed. The pictures on the wall are none other than Kirk Cameron, Jack Wagner, and Don Johnson. The sunglasses were actually helping to cover up a huge bee sting that I got in my eye the week before. My face was swollen like a lollipop and I never ate anything at camp so I was beyond skinny. Other parents were a bit freaked when they saw me without the glasses. My mom's outfit is a brand called NO! My sister was wearing ID. And what you can't see on me are my absolutely adorable Firecracker short-shorts that match the red tank. I lived for that outfit. I was nine years old.

Gabbi Robinson, Timber Ridge, Highview, WV
1986

A picture of my brother Gabe wearing his MODEL ROCKETRY IS FUN T-shirt. You probably can't tell, but my mother is taking out a box of stationery that she had bought for me, which is "Ziggy" rainbow.

Jenny Wiener, Camp Emerson, Hinsdale, MA
1978

This was an annual tradition on Visiting Day. The creative arts staff would keep the theme of the board each year a secret. Throughout the day, there would be a line of families waiting to get a snapshot behind the boards—dads with their video cameras strung around their necks, moms with their fanny packs, and girls plotting how they were going to hide all the Pringles and Coca-Cola cans that they had received that day. My dad not only was a sport but often the ringleader of these pictures every year.

Lori Harrison, Camp Romaca, Hinsdale, MA
1989–91

It was not till I went there that I realized how loosely connected our family was. How strained our family's sense of communication was. Visiting Day unwittingly provided a benchmark for judging your own family.

Jon Steingart, Camp Hess Kramer, Malibu, CA

The hardest part of Visiting Day was less that you had to be on your best behavior, and more that you had to instantly give up the foul language. It took me two weeks to detox from saying *fuck* and *shit* once I got home. Visiting Day was cold turkey.

David Lubliner, Camp Tomahawk, Bristol, NH

This is Visiting Day from summer 1983, and my mom and dad are flanking me with the Fullers, who were Miami boys like myself.

Adam Epstein, Camp Akiba, Reeders, PA 1983

Mom, Dad, and Scott on Camp Street: having just reached puberty, I was wondering how my dad ever got my mom.

Scott Jacoby
Camp Greylock, Becket, MA
1982

This moose head was put out for Visiting Day only. The camp director, Dan Bernheim, would set up a speaker inside the moose's mouth and create the effect that it could talk. He would welcome the parents through it. The moose has since been lost, and the tradition disappeared with it.

Ellen Schweber
Camp Danbee, Hinsdale, MA
1978

My parents were always late. Without fail. They flew in instead of driving and would arrive in a bizarre, Maine-inappropriate rental car. Something like a Lincoln Continental, totally unsuited to the Maine dirt roads. Three hours of Visiting Day had already gone by. The sight of hundreds of kids greeting their parents had reduced us to nervous wrecks. And then they would arrive. Dad in his khaki shorts with loafers and socks pulled up to midcalf. Mom in Ralph Lauren shorts and a blue chambray shirt. I would be sobbing as I ran up to my mom. My sister and my dad would stand there awkwardly looking at us hugging. The big deal of Visiting Day was what your family brought you for the picnic. Families became the stuff of legend for the quality and the quantity of the pastrami, heavenly cookies, or smoked salmon they would schlep up. My parents were more into quantity than quality. They bought pizza and a sub or two from the local variety store before arriving at camp. We were known for "the pile"—all of us falling asleep on each other after gorging ourselves.

Vanessa Kroll, Camp Walden, Denmark, ME
1987

DAY TRIP

I Want to Break Free

> "I've got to break free
> God knows, God knows I want to break free"
> —Queen

Deep-sea divers, miners, and astronauts are forced to decompress gradually before returning to land so as to avoid the dreaded bends, the symptoms of which include dizziness, confusion, and incontinence. Campers going on day trips received no such precautionary treatment, and as a result the outcomes of their reimmersion into the real world were uncontrollable, unpredictable, and often harmful to their health.

The day started with high spirits. As peerless an experience as camp was, it felt oh so good to leave it on a day trip, be it to the "big city" or to the kind of shabby amusement park where fatalities were a regular part of the summer. The venue was irrelevant. What mattered to the campers was the freedom. They arrived like sailors on shore leave. Ears were pierced, hair was dyed, and temporary tattoos were applied. The counselor-camper ratio, which worked fine at camp, was hopelessly inadequate back in civilized society. Anarchy ensued as kids hunting in packs quickly realized there were few consequences for mooning in the outside world.

In the afternoon, fluorescent fanny packs were emptied of all dollars in exchange for posters of seminaked ladies, T-shirts with bunk slogans spray-painted on them, and, oddly enough given that it's the most popular arts and crafts activity at any camp, more tie-dye. The day culminated in a mass pigout as the campers gorged themselves on caramel apples, cotton candy, outsize sundaes, Slurpees, or any foodstuff verboten at camp, safe in the knowledge that whatever they could stuff in their mouths had two hours to work its way back up on the bus ride home.

Stacy Bass
Pierce Camp Birchmont
Wolfeboro, NH
1978

Every two weeks we would go to the roller-skating rink, which was so old-school. Sitting together on the bus on the way there was further proof that you were indeed going out. The rink had a Slush Puppie machine, which was like a low-rent Slurpee. We would line up to buy them as if they were exotic drinks.

Jenny Weiner, Camp Emerson, Hinsdale, MA

Traditionally, our big day trip was to the Basketball Hall of Fame in Springfield, as one of our camp founders was legendary baller Nat Holman. When it was our turn to go we persuaded them to take us to the wrestling match instead at the Albany Armory. We hung around the dressing rooms after the bout—picture a dozen fifteen-year-olds trying to fit in—in an effort to persuade the noted heel Waldo Von Erich himself to come back to camp with us.

Manny Toonkle, Camp Scatico, Elizaville, NY

Debbie Shell
Camp Walden, Cheboygan, MI
1990

I grew up in New York and went to camp in central Maine, nine miles away from my family summer home on the same lake. I always felt that if times really got tough I could walk home, though nine miles might as well have been 3,000 to a ten-year-old. I convinced the camp to let my bunk go on a field trip to my family's summer home and used the trip as a ruse to lobby to stay home and not return to camp. It did not work.

**Courtney Holt (far left), Camp Takajo, Naples, ME
1979**

Wendy, Sandy, Wendy, Lisa, '82. I can still remember being slightly peeved that I was not invited to join the Martian clique that summer during our annual trip to Mackinac Island.

Liz Stevens
Camp Walden, Cheboygan, MI
1982

227

We went to Montreal in our senior year. We checked into our motel. I looked out of the window and saw a man and a woman stark naked doing it in the apartment block opposite. My whole bunk was plastered against the window aghast, staring at this act, wondering whether this was a good omen for our overnight. We invented a song for every trip, all loosely based on the same theme—about how we weren't going to take a shit till we were back at camp.

Dana Kroll, Camp Walden, Denmark, ME

You could get anything ironed onto a foam gimme cap on Mackinac Island. And we did.

Liz Stevens, Camp Walden, Cheboygan, MI
1982

The Montreal tittie bar was a rite of passage. Kids would go in and get a lesbian shower dance. I got a note in there saying meet me outside if you want a blow job. I slipped out the back and a large Chinese man was standing there, waiting for me.

Brad Feldman, Camp Greylock, Becket, MA

Every day trip starts the same—anticipation and high hopes—and ends the same—with someone throwing up all over the bus window on the way home.

Roger Bennett, Camp Kingswood, Bridgton, ME
1990

DAY TRIP

BY ANDREW GOLDBERG

Trip day. That glorious day. For us young men at Camp Wildwood in Bridgton, Maine, it was Thursdays. And it was our chance to briefly escape the artificial world of camp, enter the real world, and act like complete fucking jerks. Although every trip was accompanied by a sense of mayhem and destruction, I have culled from the annals a handful of stories in order to properly explicate and illustrate the four levels of jerkiness that only a bunk of boys on a camp trip, if properly motivated and caffeinated, can achieve.

Level one: You find rules and break them. When we were thirteen, we took a day trip to Attitash Waterslides (they also had an alpine slide, which, in terms of your chances of needing skin grafts, is about as safe as cooking meth). We went to Attitash every summer, and invariably a few kids would get thrown out of the park, usually for going down a slide two or three people at a time (apparently, this was dangerous because you could get a concussion or drown or something—I never really paid attention). But at thirteen, our entire group managed to get thrown out of the park, as not only did we go down a slide about twenty-five people at a time, but our counselor, Henry, also grabbed the female lifeguard and pulled her down with us. The folks at Attitash were so furious, our camp director made us write apology letters to avoid a camp-wide ban. Henry's letter, which he proudly read out to us before sticking it in the envelope, went something like this (as you read, imagine this is written with a pencil held tightly in his fist, so as to appear to be the musings of a young retarded boy): "Dear Attitash, I love you. What I do? I'm sorry. Love, Henry." The postscript to this story is that the final time I went to Attitash, I was a seventeen-year-old counselor and went with my friend Danny Mishkin, his older brother, and their seventy-five-year-old grandfather. And we all got thrown out of the park. Including Grandpa Mishkin.

Andrew Goldberg
Camp Wildwood
Bridgton, ME
1990

Level two: You do things your parents wouldn't normally let you do. That same summer, we went on a three-day adventure to Bar Harbor, Maine. Bar Harbor is a small coastal town with a few beaches, a boardwalk, and about thirty stores that sell wool ponchos and water bongs, and . . . pierce ears. This last item is the service that about half of my thirty fellow campers chose to indulge in because it was the early nineties, and my fellow campers were all pretty intent on looking like little Jewish LL Cool J's. In reality, though, they looked much more like Brian Austin Green. And when our group returned to camp and word spread to the culprits' parents . . . well, let's just say the phone lines between New York and Maine were burning up that evening. I can't remember exactly what their punishment was, but I imagine it was something creative, like helping our camp's three-hundred-and-fifty-pound caretaker, Bear, haul firewood. Or wax his back.

Level three: You act like animals. The following summer, we took a deep-sea fishing trip to Massachusetts. And while I was spared seasickness, having spent many childhood vacations on my family's sailboat, most of my group succumbed to the rolling waves and spent more time depositing vomit into the ocean than withdrawing fish. But that was nothing compared to the van ride back home. It all started when we stopped at McDonald's. About fifteen minutes later, Ben Berg puked in his french-fry container. We all laughed at him, but suddenly Cody Campbell's laughter turned into puking as well. This created a chain reaction whereby, not unlike a series of dominoes toppling each other one by one, all but three members of our eleven-person van were retching into various McDonald's containers (Morgan Spurlock, eat your heart out). I myself recall scurrying to the back of the van and hiding among our backpacks until the symphony of spew died down. We called it "Vomit-Palooza."

And finally, once you reach a certain age, level four: You behave like perverts. When we were fifteen, we took our senior camp trip to Quebec, Canada. It was in Quebec that I visited my first nudie bar. What kind of nudie bar, you may ask, would admit four fifteen-year-old boys? A particularly sleazy one, is the answer. To the best of my memory, the women weren't very good-looking, but they were naked, and we were fifteen, and hey, it was a nudie bar. So we sat down, ordered a bunch of Cokes with ice (we were too scared to order alcoholic drinks, and I think our skanky, six-months-pregnant waitress may have muttered the French word for "pussies" under her breath), and watched the women dance to Color Me Badd's "I Wanna Sex You Up." (Incidentally, those in our group who looked too young to get into the strip club spent the evening beating off in coin-operated peep-show stalls around the corner. Quebec

Board of Tourism, I am available to write ad copy, and I await your phone call.) Meanwhile, back at the nudie bar, after a remarkably awkward hour and a half, my friend Jeff (I've changed his name, because . . . well, you'll see) decided to get himself a lap dance. It was a fine dance, and this was Quebec in the early nineties, so it was totally nude, and by God if Jeff didn't splooge in his pants. Yup. Right at the table, in front of everyone. And the funny thing is, Jeff was kind of proud of it. And I guess in our own strange, hormonally dizzy, fifteen-year-old way, we were proud too. Jeff had reached the fourth level of jerkiness (albeit in his pants, in front of a bar full of French Canadians). He was now officially a jerk.

And these experiences, I will venture, are not unique to myself and my friends from Camp Wildwood. I am an adult now, about to get married, and I plan to send my future sons to camp. And I fully expect them to get thrown out of water parks, pierce their ears, vomit in McDonald's containers, and ejaculate in their pants. In short, to act like jerks. And if I have daughters . . . well then, I guess they'll have lesbian encounters. Because according to everything I've read in *Penthouse Forum,* that's what happens at girls' camps.

Rick Wisniewski
Camp Walden
Cheboygan, MI
1987

233

We went to see *The Karate Kid* at the mall. I found this headband in a store and was the envy of the whole camp once we had seen the movie.

**Kevin Harrison
Camp Sequoia
Rock Hill, NY
1984**

We were sixteen years old and had finally made it to counselor status. These two girls in the photo with me had been in my bunk since we were about nine or ten. Every year at the end of the summer we went on the "big trip," a four-day disaster in Ocean City, Maryland, with minimal supervision. You can imagine the amount of crap we would acquire. This year we went straight to the T-shirt shop. These girls were the sisters I never had and we wanted to express it in our clothing.

Stacy Marcus, Camp Log-N-Twig, Dingman's Ferry, PA
1986

Stocking up on softcore porn at
Orchard Beach, Maine.

**Nigel Bennett
Camp Kingswood
Bridgton, ME
1986**

Misty Mountain Hop

> "So I'm packing my bags for the Misty Mountains
> Where the spirits go now"
> —Led Zeppelin

The overnight trip was often compulsory at camp. Truth be told, campers were not always thrilled to be dragged away from the home comforts of the bunks for a hike in the mountains or a canoe trip down the rapids, but their complaints about how their parents did not pay a fortune to send them to camp so they could sleep in the leaves among bear droppings fell on deaf ears.

You would set out in a van before dawn, having been divided into groups by how fast you could go—quick, medium, and obese. The atmosphere was often funereal at the prospect of the slog ahead. The only sound to be heard was that of grumbling at the specter of half-cooked food, leaky tents, and having to take a dump in the woods. This moaning increased once the hike started until that moment when the group broke through the tree line just as the sun was rising and, for the first time, were able to view the entire valley floor below. At that precise second, it clicked into focus why you had come, and that you would not want to be anywhere else in the world but on top of that mountain right then. Carving your name on a rock at the peak, you would swear to each other that you would sign up for the overnight hike next year.

Pine Forest Camp
Greeley, PA
c. 1980

237

I took my campers on an overnight trip. We embarked on a five-hour drive out into the wilderness of Baxter State Park. But just the very night before, I had started dating a girl, and on the drive I had that indescribable next-morning thrill and could not stop thinking about her. Somewhere along the way, it dawned on me that I simply could not be away from her. And so, after abandoning the kids deep in the mountains at eleven o'clock at night, I decided to race back to camp and surprise her. I set off on the five-hour return trip only to discover that after driving all day, I could not keep my eyes open. I had been driving for roughly ten minutes when I drove straight into a tree. I was so exhausted that I hit the accelerator and wedged the bus in even farther. I had no option but to walk back to the campsite, which meant making my way through the forest in the pitch black, feeling the trees to find the way. When I got back to my kids, I was their counselor but I was the one who was sobbing.

David Wain, Camp Modin, Belgrade, ME

A girl—one who had been rumored to have slept with people—brazenly climbed into my sleeping bag on an overnight. I was so mortifyingly embarrassed by my hard-on that I kept my back to her all night long and tried to feel her up backwards. I still thought the penis was inserted perpendicularly at that time. So I was terrified that if I turned around it would slip right in.

Alex Grossman, Camp Tamarack, Ortonville, MI

Tom Rosenberg
Camp Scatico
Elizaville, NY
c. 1979

This was a camp canoe trip. I tipped over in one set of rapids and really ate it, even though I was quite a good steerer:

Claire Zulkey, Camp Echo, Fremont, MI
1992

We would canoe topless. Partly for the thrill, partly to get a tan. Down massive Maine rivers. Twelve fourteen-year-old girls in kayaks, canoeing the rapids naked.

Vanessa Kroll
Camp Walden, Denmark, ME

The line between the boys' and girls' side of camp was like the Mason-Dixon line. Or more accurately, the Maginot line in that it was impressive on paper but it did not hold. We were camping out one night . . . boys and girls in sleeping bags. I was by Missy. I had never met her before. Let's make out, she says to me. So we do just that. I was twelve. I woke up at dawn. Missy was fast asleep. This was way before roofies. I know this is wrong, but I decide I just have to put my hand down her pajamas. So I reach into her sleeping bag and slide my hand inside her pajamas and feel the cold hard steel of a metal rod. Copping a feel for the first time, I am left fondling a scoliosis brace.

David Kohan, Camp Hess Kramer, Malibu, CA

Every Day I Write the Book

"All your compliments and your cutting remarks
Are captured here in my quotation marks"
—Elvis Costello

William Randolph Hearst was reputed to have devoted his life to becoming a media magnate partly for the sake of having something to do, and partly to further his political ambitions. Both of these motivations were not so different from those who entered the world of camp media. The competition to spend the summer running the newspaper or the camp radio station was rarely fierce. Most campers preferred to dedicate their lives to the pursuit of athletic or artistic brilliance, or, failing that, to just hanging out in the sun down at the waterfront. But the reward for the camp diarist was great in terms of the raw power the position offered. Mark Twain's advice to never pick a fight with someone who buys their ink by the barrel, remained true for those who bought by the case the purple mimeograph ink that camp newsletters were cranked out with. These mini-Murdochs had the power to write annoying bunk mates out of camp history, and the power to rig the annual vote for camp's "Most Popular," "Best Looking," and "Sexiest Smile."

Camp radio was normally a shoestring operation that was constantly in flux. Beloved by the campers as an outlet for creativity, the radio station was a breeding ground for comedic campers driven by the belief that it was a small step from cracking their peers up on the airwaves to doing voiceover work for *The Simpsons*. But for the camp powers that be, radio was most often an irritant they were forced to tolerate while policing infractions such as gratuitous cursing or impersonating the camp deputy director in a derogatory fashion. Thus, the radio station spent the summer being shut down and started up as often as dissident radio in 1970s East Berlin.

Camp Henry James
Utica, MS
c. 1979

Camp Ramaquois
Pomona, NY
c. 1981

PHOTOGRAPHY!
GYMNASTICS!
COMPUTER

Camp Ramah
Grenada Hills, CA
c. 1981

I ran a radio show on the camp station, Hot 64 WJBH. The camp radio director had just killed himself, and so we had creative freedom. I invented the Camp Countdown, where my count down to zero was the signal for every bunk to flush their toilets, causing a massive plumbing problem.

Ross Martin, Camp Harlam, Kresgeville, PA

The camp newspaper was weekly. The deadline pressure felt immense as I was sent off to interview someone important like the lady who ran the pottery kiln. Everything had to be cordoned off after typing it in a square. We would hand them out fresh off the press, and they smelled so great everyone would just stand there inhaling them.

Jon Steingart, Camp Hess Kramer, Malibu, CA

THE MOGUL OF MUSKOKA

How One Woman with a Clipboard and a Dream Became the Rupert Murdoch of Camp Winnebagoe

BY RACHEL SKLAR

I spent twelve summers at Camp Winnebagoe—twenty-four months of my life, two full years, from ages twelve to twenty-three. Nestled on the shores of Fox Lake in the leafy, lake-dotted region of Muskoka in Ontario, Canada, Winnebagoe was a veritable self-contained city of four hundred of your closest friends from age eight to their midtwenties, depending on how reluctant you were to join the workforce and grow up. I was one of the latter, pushing my eighth year on staff at age twenty-three, my last summer before taking a Real Job at a law firm.

Apart from being a jewel of a place, on a sparkling lake with sun-dappled, tree-lined paths and activities like horseback riding, ceramics, tennis, water sports, and riflery (which I made a point of loudly and self-righteously eschewing all through my camp career), Winnebagoe was a place rife with overachievers. The star culture there was off the charts: Being the lead in the play, the star of the baseball team, or the pump-up counselor who dominated the mike in the dining hall—these were the things that got you noticed. I was no athlete, but I never met a mike I didn't like, or an all-day program that wasn't worth pulling an all-nighter for. Suffice it to say, my naturally dorky overachieving inclinations had the freedom to run wild.

Thus, in my twelve summers at camp, I figured out that I liked to do a lot of things, and in my final few summers, I somehow managed to do them all.

Simultaneously. In a job that, frankly, almost killed me but was probably the most fulfilling total creative experience of my life: Being the media mogul of Camp Winnebagoe. My title was "Entertainment and Media Coordinator"—fancy, right?—and here's what the job consisted of:

- As Head of Drama, directing or overseeing five full-length musicals
- Writer, editor, and publisher of the weekly camp newspaper, *The Winnebugler*
- Programming the camp radio station, W-I-N-N Winny Radio
- Videotaping all the camp events and then editing them into a weekly half-hour clip show, "This Week at Winny," as well as producing the final video for the summer
- Being on Head Staff, which meant running programs and shows and the like, plus more generally, writing songs, skits, cheers, and Serious, Moving Things to say at Friday night services

If my teenage pretensions to such a media monopoly sound like classic resume-plumping run amok, make no mistake: All of the above were vital elements of camp mogulry. Five shows. Eight videos. Eight "newspapers" (all the news that was fit to print, which happened, coincidentally, to overlap exactly with all the stuff I saw fit to write).

I didn't embark on my camp career in an obsessive quest to control the world—though of course that, like getting highlights without Sun-In, was a pleasant by-product. When I arrived at Winnebagoe in July 1985—a twelve-year old, 98-pound, boob-free beanpole following her big brother from another camp—the only thing I wanted was to make friends, water-ski, and have fun. And be the lead in the play. And write songs. And have a boyfriend. And get my period. Well, I did write songs. It took me all of about two hours to decide that Camp Winnebagoe was the greatest place on earth, during which time I scored a great bed, heard a boy thought I was cute, and fell in love with my counselor. All of which set me up for a camp career of unparalleled joy and delight and comfort in a place where I felt I could really do anything, and pretty much did.

Rachel Sklar
Camp Winnebagoe
Muskoka, ON
Canada
1991

My path to moguldom was through the drama department. Once I had a few years as Head of Drama under my belt, I figured out something interesting: Casting a camp play gave me ultimate power. Who would shine in the limelight? Who would sing the song that would bring down the house? Who would be a *star*? This all fell to me to decide. But that influence ran much further than just the leads—the true possibilities lay on the margins. Which kid was new and homesick? Which kid had failed his white tag swim test four times and needed a boost? Which kid had impetigo and was being teased by his cabin mates? Here was where I discovered the power of the cast list, how much of a difference a hastily created star turn could make, how much it mattered having a name and not just being "Chorus" (or "Angry, Torch-Wielding Mob," as I enjoyed calling a group of eight-year-olds for *Beauty and the Beast* in 1992). It was a rush, seeing a kid go from being the cabin loner to swaggering around in the spotlight based on my casting him as, say, the Lonely Goatherd in *The Sound of Music* (a vital, if completely yodeled, role).

Once drunk with this power of possibility, I couldn't help but take it further. There I was with my clipboard in one hand and my trusty Sony Handycam in the other, as much obsessed with the roller-hockey playoff and capturing the perfect flier off the water-ski docks as I was with getting the girls for "Beauty School Dropout" in a perfect V and working around the breaking voice of my thirteen-year-old Tony in *West Side Story*.* This was an altogether different type of rush—not only was I able to finally celebrate the tone-deaf kids, but I faced a new creative challenge, free of the constraints of the Rodgers & Hammerstein songbook. Every Sunday night, the entire camp would file into the theater to sit down for my version of "This Week at Winny"—what I thought was important enough for them to see, the rest of the week lost and insignificant on the cutting-room floor.

Then, of course, there was print: Something to hold on to and pore over and sneak home in your suitcase along with letters from your BFF at another camp and your Prom Card (a camp tradition: At the final social, you signed up your dances beforehand, up to twenty. Your number twenty meant *everything*). I pulled an all-nighter for *The Winnebugler* every week without fail, writing, cutting, pasting, and photocopying in the office as the sun came up. The gossip section was positively devoured every week, in between articles about camp events like the Psychic Fair ("'I Knew You'd Say That,' Says Mysterious

* You don't realize how many goddamned *Maria*s there are in that song until you've heard it from a painfully pubescent thirteen-year-old. There are twenty-eight. Say it soft and it's almost like praying!

Stranger") and house ads begging for contributions with jokes that I am both embarrassed and proud to admit I still use today ("Write for *The Winnebugler!* You Don't Need to Know No Grammar Or How to Spel!").

Between the plays, videos, and *'Bugler* I admit that I left the radio station woefully underprogrammed, except for running audio of camp shows and turning the mike over to the teen boys' cabins to play their gangsta rap. Ah, well, everything at camp has its place.

Mostly, my media machinations were benign; I will, however, cop to taking a bit of savage satisfaction from using my power to strike back at someone who had pissed me off. (All's fair in love and color war, people.) Camp can be a competitive place, particularly when you stock it with a bunch of high-achievers who have grown up jockeying for position with each other every summer: feuds and rivalries are bound to break out, factions to spring up. As in the rest of the world, sex and politics were never far away, idyllic though the setting may have been. Sometimes, all it took to shift the fault lines and allegiances was a night hooking up in the ski shed or rolling around on the stage at Chapel Point. (Not that I ever did *that*. The ski shed totally had bugs.) But, you know, that made for a pretty good lesson for a budding media mogul: That there was power, but there was also accountability and responsibility. Sure, I could cut my nemesis out of the video and stick him in the chorus, but for what? The cheap thrill of victory wrung from abuse of position? What was I, a Republican? The real loser in that scenario would be me—because that nemesis had a good voice, and the kids loved him, and he made for good video.

Even the most inveterate camper has to grow up sometime, so eventually I left Winnebagoe behind, sort of. I say "sort of" because its lessons have stayed with me, though I no longer have as many opportunities to write songs rhyming "cavort" and "sport." The big takeaway from my summers of being the Clear Channel of Camp Winnebagoe was that, man, was I ever lucky. Not only did I have the chance to make shows and videos and awesome memories out of thin air, but I got to do it with amazing, talented kids and staff members, the kind that could alternately tap-dance and go up on pointe or sit down at a piano and figure out a song by ear in 0.5 seconds, or stay up all night to write a completely original tune that used guitar, bass, keyboards, cowbell, and three-part harmony, or tinker around in a room with wires for a few hours and emerge triumphant with a radio frequency. I can't think of any summer job that could have done more for me as a writer, or an artist, or a collaborator. To this day, I count as one of my greatest accomplishments the mounting of *Grease Two*—in what *has* to have been the only stage version ever—with Rollerblades standing in for motorcycles, and a giant ramp leading up to the stage from the audience. (The lawyer in me cringes now at the thought of fourteen-year-old boys doing wheelies over the heads of trusting eight-year-olds, but the artist in me was thrilled.) That's my great memory, but it's one I share with all the kids in that show who learned their lines and songs and choreography—and at a place like Winnebagoe, those were the memories that were made by everyone, every day, on the field or on water skis or in talent shows or, yes, rolling around on the stage at Chapel Point. It was my great gift to be the chronicler of such things, my great honor to be a collaborator in them. Let the other media moguls grab for the power—I'm content to hold on to the memories.

Camp Ramah
Grenada Hills, CA
c. 1982

I had a crush on a girl and dedicated "Right Here Waiting" by Richard Marx to her. The broadcast signal was not so great, so I taped myself doing this and went around to her bunk and played it for her on a cassette player. We went out for two very awesome days.

Simmy Kunstawitz, Camp Ramah in the Berkshires, Wingdale, NY

Fire and Rain

> "I've seen fire and I've seen rain
> I've seen sunny days that I thought would never end"
> —James Taylor

Our prehistoric ancestors' discovery of fire 1.7 million years ago is widely heralded as the most critical breakthrough in the history of humanity: cooking, heating, and metalworking are some of the many vaunted innovations that resulted. But arguably the most important contribution it made to civilization was enabling the ritual of the bonfire at the American summer camp. Or so it felt when you were sitting around the campfire, resplendent in a Day-Glo T-shirt with a bandanna on your head. Under the stars in the great outdoors, it was as if you were living history. The campfire was the place where you were most connected to all campers past, who had sat at the same spot, singing similar songs and performing the same rituals so sensitively adapted from Indian lore.

Every bunk had the opportunity to invent its own fire song, a creative act that involved plagiarizing a popular melody—Rod Stewart's "Forever Young" was much in demand—and melding it with new lyrics that relied on the desperate overuse of metaphors to address the grave sadness that was impossible for the human heart to bear triggered by the prospect of leaving camp at the end of the summer. As you sang the lines, the pressure was immense. You knew the popularity of your bunk would be made evident if others remembered your lyrics and repeated them at the next campfire, forging a new link in the chain of camp tradition, aka immortality.

Ian Cohen
Camp Cedar Lake,
Milford, PA
1986

251

The huge campfire every Saturday evening was the most anticipated night of the week because of the sketches, songs, and dances we would perform. The oldest campers were in charge of hosting the acts. We decided to take this to a new level by dressing as nerds and completely taking over the night's set list. This was one of the most formative nights of our lives.

Josh Lewis, David Berger, Joey Garfield, Todd Hasak-Lowy
Habonim Camp Tavor, Three Rivers, MI
1985

Campfire meant council affairs. Three times each summer, the whole camp came together to read poems, with you and your best friend swapping off every other line. It was all very solemn stuff featuring songs about friendship, nature, and the beauty of north Minnesota. The culmination was us cross-connecting arms to sing about the whispering of the trees and the haunting melodies.

Katie Rosman, Camp Thunderbird, Bemidji, MN

Our camp was all about history and tradition. You knew your history. You could say "1968" and we would know who was team leader and what their cheers were. Sometimes these old campers would come back to visit and it was as if a celebrity had arrived. We were so in awe of them. We knew their songs. When you sat around the campfire, it was as if you were living history. The camp kept a record of all the news read out at campfire. And you were aware that you were sitting in the same spot in the same way as girls had since WWII.

Rachel Kane, Camp Che-Na-Wah, Minerva, NY

Traditional Indian ceremony.

Camp Tamakwa, Algonquin Park, ON, Canada
1975

Traditional Noon-Way "Initiation of the Camp Season" ceremony conducted on the first night of every summer, asking the great spirit of Wakonda for a blessing for the new camp season.

Camp Tamakwa
Algonquin Park, ON, Canada
1979

Our camp ran on a system of false reward. Every camper got a lanyard on the first day they arrived. They were just plastic beads. But they meant everything. You would kill for these beads and devoted the rest of the summer to building up a collection.

Red was for land sports.
Blue was for water sports.
Yellow was for cleanliness—collective bunk cleanliness.
Green or white was given to you free upon your arrival—like a drug dealer, the first hit is free.

The beads were given out at a council fire every Saturday night. We would sit in tribes on logs, the fire's sparkle reflecting off our hairless legs that glistened with Off spray. Green tribe on one log. The white on another. And play games you should never play by a fire while wearing 100 percent polyester: like an invented game that would often have us rolling around in the dirt in our sweatshirts. Or potato sack races.

Sloane Crosley, Camp Wa-Klo, Keane, NH
1989

INDIAN LORE

The Indian Lore program seeks to give campers an appreciation for the crafts and culture of the American Indian. Boys learn to make Indian crafts from natural materials and create their own costumes and weapons for a special Indian Campfire presented at the end of our Main Session. Indian teas, dinners and overnights are held at the authentic bark house and tepee in the Indian Village.

Orinoco Flow

"Let me sail, let me sail,
Let me crash upon your shore"
—Enya

The waterfront was more than a front of activity; it was a prism through which the social and political hierarchies of camp were revealed in the light of day for all to see. Yes, there were the die-hard swimmers, led by their role model, the camp *Man from Atlantis,* the director of water sports; and the avid water-skiers, who dedicated their lives religiously to mastering the mono-ski and attracting the attention of those divine biological specimens, the Australian counselors driving the motorboat. But the more interesting activities took place onshore, in a scene that looked as if *Sports Illustrated* had decided to do an adolescent swimsuit edition. Luminous Body Glove bikinis and OP board shorts showcased the limbs of the beautiful. If you had it, you flaunted it, be it chest hair or breasts. Those without cowered at the fringes, covering chests with baggy T-shirts and cloaking legs in beach towels.

Tom Rosenberg
Camp Scatico
Elizaville, NY
c. 1978

Karen Laureston
KenWood Camp, Kent, CT
1988

BLOB

Literally, the blob is an inflatable piece of plastic, eighteen feet long and seven feet high. You jumped off the high dive (shown in the upper left section of photo) and onto the blob. If (and I stress if) you landed successfully, you then moved to the back of the blob, stood up, and waited for the next kid to jump. If the kid was bigger than you, you'd get tossed into the air and either land back onto the blob or fall into the lake.

Figuratively, the blob was many of my fears rolled into one. The first day of my first year at camp I tried jumping onto the blob, somehow missed almost entirely, hit the back of my neck on the ropes that secure the blob to the lake bottom, and almost drowned (exaggeration). I came up above water to the sound of forty other boys laughing at me. Maybe it was because I just solidified myself as a spaz or maybe it was because I had ripped the new pair of Jams shorts my mom had bought for me before camp. Needless to say, I spent a lot of time in arts and crafts that summer.

Perry Silver, Falling Creek Camp, Tuxedo, NC
1987

Blair and Mitchell are seated, judging the "muscle contest" on the girls' side waterfront. For a boy like me all of that adolescent and teenage flesh stuffed into Speedos was quite an eyeful to behold.

Laser Rosenberg,
Camp Modin, Belgrade, ME
1981

Townsend Dam. It was close to the camp and we'd go on overnight outings there. That was the only time I wore shoes that summer, ever. And only 'cause they made us when we left the campgrounds so they didn't get shut down by the health department. Perfection was nabbing one of the inner tubes before they were monopolized by the older kids.

Amy Blackman
Heart's Bend Camp, Newfane, VT
1979

YOU HAVE NOW EARNED YOUR CERTIFICATE— PIN—EMBLEM!

17. COMBINED SKILLS CHECK

16. SAFETY SKILLS

15. JUMPING IN

14. DIVING

So Shari and I were wakeboarding. I think that's what we called it—it's like windsurfing without the sail, which they felt we were too young for. We hated the lake, the fish, and the seaweed, and the cold. We used to say we had stomachaches, colds, periods (which neither of us had yet)—anything to get out of having to go in.

Ariel Silberman
Camp Echo Lark, Poyntelle, PA
1986

That's me in front of Long Lake using my T-shirt to cover my Speedo. This is my "Splash Asch" T-shirt. I thought of myself as a freshwater superhero but I also had my "Flash Asch" T-shirt for out-of-water activities. One of my counselors called me "Hash Asch." I thought he meant potatoes; he probably was thinking brownies.

Kevin Asch, Camp Takajo, Naples, ME
1985

Caren Cohen
Point O'Pines,
Brant Lake, NY
1978

Two Tribes

"When two tribes go to war
A point is all you can score"
—Frankie Goes to Hollywood

On the eve of the Allied invasion of France, General Patton inspired his troops by reminding them that "all real Americans love the sting of battle. When you were kids, you all admired the champion marble shooter, the fastest runner, the big league ball players, the toughest boxers . . . Americans love a winner and will not tolerate a loser." A more succinct paraphrase of this would be "1-2-3-4, we want a Color War! 5-6-7-8, we don't want to wait!"

There is nothing like a Color War. All of the compassion and sharing that had been cultivated so tenderly from the very first day of camp was thrown away in the instant it took to fire the Color War cannon. Friendships were either forgotten or transformed into scores that had to be settled. The camp that had been a community was splintered into factions hell-bent on destroying each other. And every camper became gripped by a mix of seething hatred, urgency, commitment, passion, and desperate fear of failure. Color War was gut-check time; it was the Olympics, the Grammys, and a spelling bee, rolled into one.

A series of "fake-outs" finally gave way to the "breakout." The themes were announced, the captains were selected, and the teams were organized. And then the games began. You gave it your all to ensure victory, with a combination of athleticism, spirit, and your ability to stay up all night and write new lyrics to popular songs and then sing them with voices hoarse from cheering your Ping-Pong team to victory. Color War could make or break you. A victorious captain was guaranteed a successful and happy life. But drop the baton during the Apache relay and flunking out of college, going into rehab, and working the night shift at McDonald's was most probably your future.

Roger Bennett
Camp Kingswood
Bridgton, ME
1990

Brenda Lowenberg
Camp Westmont, Poyntelle, PA
1988

Of course I was chosen to be captain. I was a closer back then. I had no fear. The only people who were physically more able than me were those individuals— every camp has one or two—who kept coming back to camp for a suspiciously long time—they had a beard and were fully developed and able to conjure up a toga for the Color Wars.

David Light, Camp Ramah in the Poconos, Lake Como, PA

We would march down in height order to perform the cheer. We were taught to march as choppily as possible. And then we cheered. The cheer would be rated both for itself and for the echo it created from the mountains.

Rachel Kane, Camp Che-Na-Wah, Minerva, NY

Our camp colors were brown, so we had two teams. One wore brown, the other tan. Team Doodie against Team Diarrhea. These are the mascots for the brown team—Bruno and Tango. Bruno and Tango met a grisly fate—they were lost in a great lice epidemic.

Dana Kroll, Camp Walden, Denmark, ME
1989

The highlight of the summer was Color War. And the most exalted position was Color War captain or general. The team leader. I had wanted to be captain since the first day I set foot in camp—the pride I experienced when I became one was palpable, because you were voted in by your peers. Achieving this was still one of the proudest moments of my young life. The culmination of our Color War was the chicken fight, in which the whole division would be in a circle hopping on one leg with the other pulled up behind your back. The aim was to bump into each other and eliminate opponents by pushing them over or making them lose their grip on their nonhopping foot. The winner was last man standing. Our strategy? Have our big guys hang back, and use the smaller boys as pawns. Traditionally, all the campers and counselors would go crazy to psych themselves up for this tournament, breaking brooms and smashing chairs, and the camp directors hated that. One summer, the Color War came down to this competition. We were up on points but it was close. Wary of the camp directors' dislike of the traditional frenzy, we elected to take our team out to the ball fields to chill out and calmly prepare for battle. This proved to be a big mistake, for when we arrived at the chicken fight circle, the other team was in a frenzy, breaking brooms and smashing chairs, and they kicked our asses.

Doug Herzog, Camp Scatico, Elizaville, NY

Our camp always had amazingly creative themes. Future versus past (breakout: a hot air balloon). Superman versus Batman (breakout: counselors zipping down gym walls on a wire). The choreography was immaculate. And then came our year: Cro-Magnons versus Neanderthals. Are you kidding me? Our Cro-Magnon costumes were burlap sacks. We looked so ridiculous I asked the camp director to explain the difference between Cro-Magnons and Neanderthals and why they would fight. They never lived at the same time. Try working "Neanderthal" into a song.

Andrew Goldberg, Camp Wildwood, Bridgton, ME

Something nice happened

To:

From:

The team captains would unveil the costumes for Color War at an evening called Team Feast. This was achieved by stripping the captain naked—butt naked—in front of the team. When you were nine years of age, to see a naked camper—a fully developed woman—was an indescribable thrill. Young girls would push to the front to see the naked girls stripped bare. Some would stand there like supermodels. Others would make a joke. Others cowered awkwardly. They would spray Soft & Dri under their arms and the spray would hang over all of us like a smog. We would sit there in quiet wonder. "Is that how my body is going to develop?" And then we would eat cake. Color War to me is all about cake and boobs.

Jordan Roter, Tripp Lake Camp, Poland, ME

WaR is iMMiNeNT

Tom Rosenberg
Camp Scatico, Elizaville, NY
c. 1978

This is the tug of war at the famed "mo and din" Color Wars. I am digging my feet in as deep as possible to pull as hard as I could. It felt like quicksand.

Laser Rosenberg
Camp Modin, Belgrade, ME
1979

269

SIX SUREFIRE RULES TO DOMINATE COLOR WAR

BY ROSS MARTIN

Becoming a general was the most important moment of my life. I was invited to a clandestine meeting in a secret corner of Camp Harlam I didn't know existed. When I arrived, seven other counselors were already there, staring at T-shirts on the wall. There were two in each color, red, green, blue and gold. Each had a name on the back. Mine said GENERAL ROSS in white letters on true green, THE CAVEMEN.

We were silent. In awe. The latest in a long line of camp's legendary Color War generals, anointed to lead teams of screaming Jewish campers to victory and . . . what? Immortality? Macabee wannabes, all of us. And then it hits you. I'm about to spend the next week of my life plotting to destroy everyone who is not wearing green.

The first job Color War generals do is actually collaborative: to figure out how to "break" Color War. The goal is simple: Set the camp on fire with the spirit of the games.

The best Color War break I'd ever seen was the year the generals literally faked a fire. They cajoled the Kunkletown fire department into allowing its klunky fire truck—the only one in the county—to show up at camp one afternoon with sirens roaring. Eight firemen jumped out, climbed atop the dining hall, and ripped off their heavy fire gear. They were our counselors, and we went wild: "R, G, B, G— RGBG!!!"

When I was a general, we went for a more conceptual approach. In the dark of night, armed with tins of fresh paint, we put a dab of color on each kid's forehead. They woke up in the morning, looked in the mirror, and realized that Color War had "broken" while they slept, they'd been drafted to teams, and how the hell did that happen?

I will now reveal to you the secrets of how to win Color War in six easy steps:

1. Draft Strategically. When negotiating with other generals as to which campers will be drafted to which teams, target the loudest, most spirited girls for your team. Sure, they will give you a headache and be annoying. But they'll lose their voices by day three and inspire the rest of the team to carry you to victory on their shoulders.

2. SPIRIT! Athletic prowess is overrated. Spirit wins you Color War. Well, perceived spirit, that is. I deputized the most innocent-looking campers on my team to be an early warning system, to march ahead and detect when roaming judges were coming near. When a judge approached, the Cavemen spontaneously erupted in a choreographed team cheer. (Note—we didn't just cheer for our team, we cheered for sports in general. A universal cheer for the glory of competition always endears you to judges.) As soon as the judge had awarded us points for great sportsmanship and moved on, it was critical to stop cheering immediately and to focus on kicking other teams' asses or, if we were losing, to throw in the towel and conserve energy.

Ross Martin
Camp Harlam
Kresgeville, PA
1992

3. Energy. Sugar, if used strategically, is your friend. Dump an extra scoop or two in each cup of bug juice. Only the dentist's kid will notice.

4. Deliberate Losing. Dump your least athletic campers into the sports you know you are going to lose anyway. But make a point of cheering for them, which will earn you sympathy (and more good sportsmanship points) from judges.

5. Clapton Gets 'Em Every Time. Same with U2, Boomtown Rats, Cyndi Lauper, and, of course, Billy Joel. The biggest night of most Color Wars is the night each team performs its Fight Song and its Alma Mater. There's one goal: jerk tears. Write songs set to tunes like "Wonderful Tonight" and change the lyrics to "This is our last camp night." Place campers most likely to experience extreme emotions at the front, and be sure to position them so the judges can see them well. Have tissues, of course, but don't take them out until the judges start crying too.

6. When You Win. Winning Color War is something you never forget. But next year, will anyone in camp remember you won? Probably not. If you want to go down in history, rip off your general shirt the minute you win, and in the glory of the moment, toss it to the smallest camper on your team, Mean Joe Greene–style. Cue sobbing campers in the front who led you to victory during your Alma Mater and even the judges will be crying. I didn't do this, so when I see old friends from camp, no one seems to remember that I led the Cavemen to victory, a regret I will carry with me to the end of my days.

We a
resul
couns
of vi
deter

Je ex

The culmination of Color War was Flag Rush, which feels like it must have taken place in another era—a prelitigation era. Our Color War elimination was a full tackle competition, not tag. There were twenty broken bones, guaranteed. The infirmary was on standby. They even had an ambulance waiting on the sidelines from the very beginning.

Matt Adler, Camp Manitou, Oakland, ME

Color War ended in a quiz. The whole thing hinged on a sudden-death round, the last question of which was aimed at me: How many tribes of Israel were there? I said thirteen. I knew I fucked up as soon as I said it. As soon as the words came out. In its wake, I was not punished by my peers per se because I had a lot of friends at camp and other than the one counselor I tortured, I was pretty well liked. But here's what I do know, I definitely punished myself. How many years ago was this? Twenty-three? I can still describe that feeling at the core of my stomach as if it were yesterday. I remember feeling like the room had literally stopped. As I am sitting here typing I am also remembering that the only other time I felt time stand still like that was when I was first diagnosed with thyroid cancer five years ago. Do you see why camp was so heinous? I equate the experience of fucking up at Color War with cancer. I guess to my thirteen-year-old self it felt like that; it was too much damn pressure.

Nancy Lefkowitz, Camp Eisner, Great Barrington, MA

y days, exhibit the
ou have received fr
l activities. The
combat, is always

sportsmanship. W
less.

a time of treme

t staggers the imagination to see the accomplishments of individuals and
ver such a short period of time.

Youngsters from 5 to
pportunities are av
hances and challenge

e all must face this
elp each other to do

he judges will provi

k yourself "What

joy yourself and
roblem.

ief Judges - E
            Je
            Ec

Color War began with breakouts—an elaborately choreographed announcement that Color was upon us. But before a breakout, there were a series of "fake-outs," which were easy to spot. Breakouts were extravagant—a helicopter flying over camp and showering us with leaflets informing us that Color War was breaking out. Fake-outs were always cheap and nasty in comparison. Leaflets given out telling us to report to a certain place at a certain time. Nothing would occur. The lameness was always a tip-off.

Mark Miller, Seneca Lake, Honesdale, PA

Our version of Color War was called College Day, where we assumed the names of the mediocre institutions of higher education that our counselors attended—we competed against teams called Rutgers and Florida International.

Jenny Weiner, Camp Emerson, Hinsdale, MA

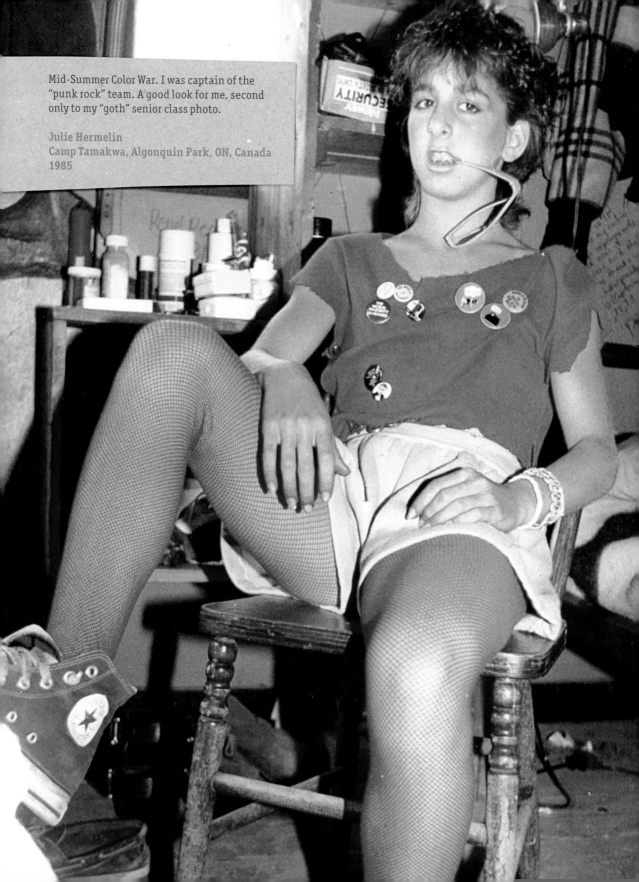

Mid-Summer Color War. I was captain of the
"punk rock" team. A good look for me, second
only to my "goth" senior class photo.

Julie Hermelin
Camp Tamakwa, Algonquin Park, ON, Canada
1985

The sport I really mastered was Ping-Pong. I dominated that table. I spent the summer quietly honing my skills for Color War—two teams, two factions really—the competition engendered such deep hatred, and Ping-Pong became a competitive sport. This was a beautiful time for the marginalized and the iconoclasts—those of us who were masters of the less popular sports—not football, baseball, basketball—to take center stage and become a prize strategic asset for the first time all summer. All those hours committed to the Ping-Pong table paid off. The same goes for those kids who were good at arts and crafts or chess. Picture thousands of kids hanging on every single move. Living and dying by every move of a pawn. That one kid's victory would score as many points as that of a victorious basketball team. At the end of Color War every kid would cry. Win or lose. Because it meant the end of camp. I never cried. I liked Color War, don't get me wrong. But I saw through it.

Scott Jacoby, Camp Greylock, Becket, MA

SILENT MEAL

First day lunch of MO and DIN is the Silent Meal competition for the upper and lower units.

The rules are as follows:

1. The old field will be split up into 2 squares marked by cones. There will be one square for each team..

2. The teams are lines up in their respective meeting places and march silently, when called, to where the Head Honchos place them.

3. No talking upon entering the dining hall (except for the blessing.)

4. The meal is buffet style.

5. No team is allowed to get its food until it is called up by the Head Honchos.
   (second helpings will be allowed, but only at the indication of the Head Honchos.)

6. Each team is expected to clean up its area. Points will be deducted if the area is not clean.

7. Silent meal ends after the Birkat.

Points are known only by Head Honchos.

SSHHHHHHHHHH !!!

My "big event" was when someone poured freezing cold water onto my head and my job was to catch it in a Mountain Dew bottle until it filled up the bottle. I am grimacing like the water is already pouring on my head and it is soooooooo cold, yet my hair and face are completely dry. That's because I knew the camp photographer was watching and I wanted to give him a good shot.

Perry Silver, Falling Creek Camp, Tuxedo, NC
1991

THE ART OF WAR

BY DAVID LUBLINER

olor War always started the same way. Three shots from a cannon. Of course, this gave rise to a series of fake-outs—like the cannon being fired at one in the morning, but only twice. It did not matter what time of day it was when those three shots rang out. We would report to the social hall, where the camp directors (Jon Small and Mike "Griff" Griffin) would be waiting. Griff would slowly and torturously divide the camp into two teams— the blue and the gray—starting with the five- and six-year-olds and, an hour later, finally reaching the older bunks. The teams themselves were brilliantly designed to be as even as possible to ensure there were no blowouts, and to maximize the possibility of a dead heat.

The identity of the Color War generals was one of the best-kept secrets of the year. Would it be a new pairing, or would it be a rematch from the previous year's gargantuan tussle? To the five-year-old campers, it did not matter— whoever was chosen looked like a god, and as soon as they were chosen the intensity of the conflict revealed itself. The blue team's general would descend from the side with hatchet in hand, screaming and yelling. Partly because he was pumped up by the honor, and partly because he knew that now he was a Color War general, the rest of his life was guaranteed to be a success.

We would then return to our bunks, knowing that for five days we would not speak to the other team, even if they were our best friends or family.

Color War was the most competitive environment I have ever encountered. Even when it came to singing. Big points were up for grabs at Song Night, when both teams performed an alma mater (rah! rah! rah!) and a fight song tailored specifically for the event. Even the act of standing up to sing had to be synchronized to score points. Both tunes were written by the team leaders to the songs of Billy Joel or Elton John and sung by the teams with no irony at all. This was a gravely serious business. Too much was at stake.

The finale was always the Round the Bases Relay. At this point in Color War, the competition was—surprise, surprise—still neck and neck, so the 50

points up for grabs were massive. Round the Bases was guaranteed to matter. It always had the feeling of a World Series game seven. In the middle of summer every camper had been timed running the bases so that each Color War team held the same amount of talent. Take into account that most of us had not slept in four nights by this point—we had been up all night writing fight songs and arguing over strategy. The stakes could not have been higher. The five top runners in each of eight age groups were entered—and if one slipped, or dropped the baton, that would mean five days of teamwork and sweat and effort and synchronized marching down the drain.

I had three wins and two losses in Color Wars, a statistic I will carry with me throughout life. The three victories were celebrated with tears of joy, the losses with tears of pain. Junior campers and twenty-year-old counselors alike were guaranteed to be sobbing whatever the result. Each of us had given our all and left it out there on the field, whether it was on the basketball court, at Song Night, or in marching two-by-two in formation around camp between events. Whatever the result, a sense of relief always kicked in once Color War was over. And although the whole camp then joined together in singing the Camp Tomahawk Fight Song, the competition had run so deep that it took hours for the camp social hierarchy to gel again. Both winners and losers would lay silent and exhausted in their bunks wrestling internally with the question "Why did I go through so much stress for this?" But the reality was that we would all throw ourselves right back into it next year, as competitively as we had over the past five days. Probably more so.

This is the Apache Bunk. I was 13 years old sporting the insanely high knee socks we were all victim to. I am second from the left. My friend Darryl Frank is holding the "Apache" sign. Paul Leibowitz is sixth from the left.

David Lubliner,
Camp Tomahawk,
Bristol, NH
1982

Camp Nebagamon's all-camp Color War was called "Pow Wow Day" (later renamed "Paul Bunyan Day" due to political correctness). Each of the teams' leaders, or Big Chiefs, represents their tribe's colors—Cherokee, Sioux, Chippewa, Navajo. Camp director Nardie Stein hands out the ceremonial battle-ax to the winning Big Chief, in recognition of the glorious competitive victory of the day.

Brice Rosenbloom
Camp Nebagamon, Lake Nebagamon, WI
1986

Brenda Lowenberg
Camp Westmont,
Poyntelle, PA
c. 1988

Hillary Auster
Camp Edward Isaacs
Holmes, NY
1985

Dear Mom, Dad

Hi! Whats up? Gess what. We Won Colorwar. White ghostbusters

The Blue Gremlins are so cute. A little girl dressed up as guizmo and she was so cute.

There has been a stomach virass gorging arousens. 5 people got in in our bunk. About 15 people got it in rebbeca. They all threw up.

I just went to lunch. Beth always goes first. I Beth went. Then Debbie says "dont go yet ruth didnt go." When I was walking to the side and then she goes to be "dont give me that snotty look" when I didnt even give her a look. look. Its not fair she tells all the counslers I lied, tells them bad things about me and, now they hate me. I relley got to go. 7 days
Love Jenna XOXOXOXO

Jenna Fallon
Camp Edward Isaacs
Holmes, NY
1985

279

Color War general for Blue Rap. We got beat real bad that year by Golden Western.

Scott Rothschild
Camp Kennybrook
Monticello, NY
1992

I was a great camper. An übercamper, once I got the hang of it. I was good at sports and that made me a natural leader. I always had a boyfriend. Toward the end of camp, when other campers had become apathetic, I still cared. I won the decathlon, starred in the musical, won the regatta against the boys' camp. So when it came to Color War and the captains were voted on by counselors—though no one quite understands what the qualifications were—I became a general. The only downside was that my cogeneral was a loser guy named Howie, with whom I was tasked to stay up all night writing fighting lyrics to Barry Manilow and Styx tunes for the Sing event, and painting banners with the original cheer, "1-2-3-4, this is Color War."

The critical event was the Apache Relay. The green and white hatchets nailed into the rec hall front door were still neck and neck. All hinged on the relay, and the last leg had the two generals swimming back to the waterfront after someone else had kayaked out with the baton. By the time I hit the water, it was all over, and we had lost. As I swam back the winning team was celebrating in the water. I swam through the celebrations and kept running when I hit the beach, back to my cabin, where I sobbed and pulled myself together for Sing, an activity I had no voice or energy left for. . . . Despite the crushing loss, Color War made me realize how to manage. How good I was at it. That you had to really want to lead, and to invest time and energy in other people.

Amy Israel, Camp Watitoh, Becket, MA

Barker Team 1977

To the tune of Hawaii- Five O

Barker team we've strived hard
to be number one
working hard together
having lot's of fun

Tennis swimming basketball too
Pep and Vim come shinning through
We're the barkers
Try with all our might-let's go

Our captains Bob & Sharon
Have led us through this week
Keeping us together
Climbing to our peak

Rubes and Clowns and Roustabouts to
Barkers wish our luck to you   tonite – figh
But the Barkers are gonna win-

To the tune of Union Lable

We are the fighting Barkers   Brown team Day
We've strived this whole week
to try to reach our goal   final

We've worked with spirit
and Pep and vim
to try to win our fight tonoght   today

And with our captains Sharon & Bob to,   And with our team we've worked hard fight
They've led us through this carnival   last year anther top

We've had so much fun
As we've reached number one
and we shall stay on top the great yellow team   milky ways

the tune of "I Did It My Way

1 The week is at an end

The fires bright
the faces glowing

2 The Barker team has strived our spirit high
the victory's showing 3the friendships we've made.
The old have stayed forever golden.   that

4 To Barkers we'll be true from here on after.
5 But Birchmont you have changedimproved and gained

A new surrounding.

6 Through all the sports we've played our pep has stayed
the fun we treasure.

7 To red & Green & Blue good luck to you
the best be with you.
8 But captains Sharon and Bob our thanks we give   you.

LAST NIGHT

I Think We're Alone Now

**"Running just as fast as we can
Holding on to one another's hand"
—Tiffany**

To everything there is a season. And camp, which had seemed an eternity at the beginning of summer, ended like the needle falling off an Aerosmith record. Once the tense action of Color War was over, the last few days of camp quickly fizzled away. Packing and cleaning were followed by a banquet dinner or awards ceremony, which served as a prelude for one last night of anarchy. With the camp Rules of Law weakened by the prospect of imminently returning home, campers would go on raids, break into the kitchen and steal ice cream, or smoke cigarettes without fear of punishment.

The boundaries between the oldest campers and the counselors were shattered at this time, as both prepared to move from one world to another. The campers would try to act blithely as they were invited into the counselor lounge to stay up late, drink beer, and share stories about which campers they liked and which they hated. Back in the bunks, other campers were throwing "sloshies," wet toilet paper, at people and property, peppering the roof of the bunks, where they would hang down and harden, a permanent testament to their warrior-ness. But there was no better way to mark territory than taking a marker, finding a clean part of the bunk wall and marking it with creative, meaningful phrases such as "Scott waz here. Summer of '86." This act was a discreet balance between visibility (it had to be seen . . .) and discretion (. . . but not so obvious that you got into trouble). Carving in your name, you felt immortal.

> On the last night of camp, we would gather around and set light to a bonfire in the shape of the year and then float candles out into the water and sing slow songs on the beach. We tried to purposefully do these things so we could cry.
>
> Rachel Kane
> Camp Che-Na-Wah
> Minerva, NY

THERE COMES A TIME
WHEN WE NEED TO BE AT CAMP.
WHEN THE MEN
MUST COME TOGETHER AS POINT
THERE ARE RUSTLERS FIGHTING
TO GO OUT WITH ALL THE POINT
TONIGHT THE GREATEST NIGHT OF ALL

EVERY BODY
BILL CAN'T GO ON
PRETENDING DAY BY DAY
THAT SOMEONE, SOMEDAY WILL SOON CLEAN
THE JOHN'S
WE'RE ALL A PART OF
BILL'S GREAT BIG FAMILY
AND THE TRUTH YOU KNOW
STAFF IS ALL WE NEED

STAFF
WE ARE THE STAFF
THESE ARE OUR CHILDREN
THEY ARE THE ONES WHO RUIN ALL OUR DAYS
SO LET'S GET GOING

CAMPERS
IT'S THE CHANCE THEY'RE TALKING
THEY'RE RISKING THEIR OWN LIVES
CAMPERS & STAFF
ITS TRUE THERE WILL BE BETTER DAYS
JUST WAIT AND SEE

JIM
WELL WE'LL EAT OUT-YOUR HEARTS
AND SHOW THAT WE DON'T CARE.
JIM & MARK
AND WE'LL DO THE FUNKY CHICKEN
THAT'S MEAN

MARK
YEAGH - BILL HAS TOLD US
NOT TO GET ANY REDS
FEDELE
BUT BILL Y-KNOW YOUR TENT
IS NEVER CLEAN
DAN
THEY ARE THE RUSTLERS
THEY ARE THE WOMEN
SKEETER
THEY ARE THE ONES WHO REALLY WANT US
SO THEY'LL START GIVING

SOLO'S

Based on
"We Are the World."

Ken Freimann
Camp Norwich
Huntington, MA
1986

Catie Lazrus
Camp Walden
Bancroft, ON, Canada
1989

This was the "banquet" that was held at the end of every summer, where we all got "dressed up" and ate "better food" and celebrated the summer behind us. The last night of the summer was the one in which everyone, not just the cool kids, stayed up all night. It was cold and we had just packed so none of us had the right clothing to stay warm. We would stand around crying. Freezing. All the girls were sobbing. This was your last chance for everything. To tell the person what you really thought of them. How much you loved them. To get a blow job. Or at the very least make out. Every place was a makeout place that night.

David Wain, Camp Modin, Belgrade, ME
1983

Our final tradition was a huge slide show of images showing every single camper in action throughout the summer. The show was really a Machiavellian popularity contest in which the campers would cheer as loud as they could for the kids they loved and met the retards with total, excruciating silence.

David Light, Camp Ramah in the Poconos
Lake Como, PA

Dear Lazer,
Well, when I first met you I thought you were a good kid, I still do. don't worry what other people say, that's not important. JUST stay good! and I'll see ya next year!
Love,
Dana

JULIE JULIE JULIE

JULIE JULIE JULIE

BANQUET '82"

I'LL MISS YOU!

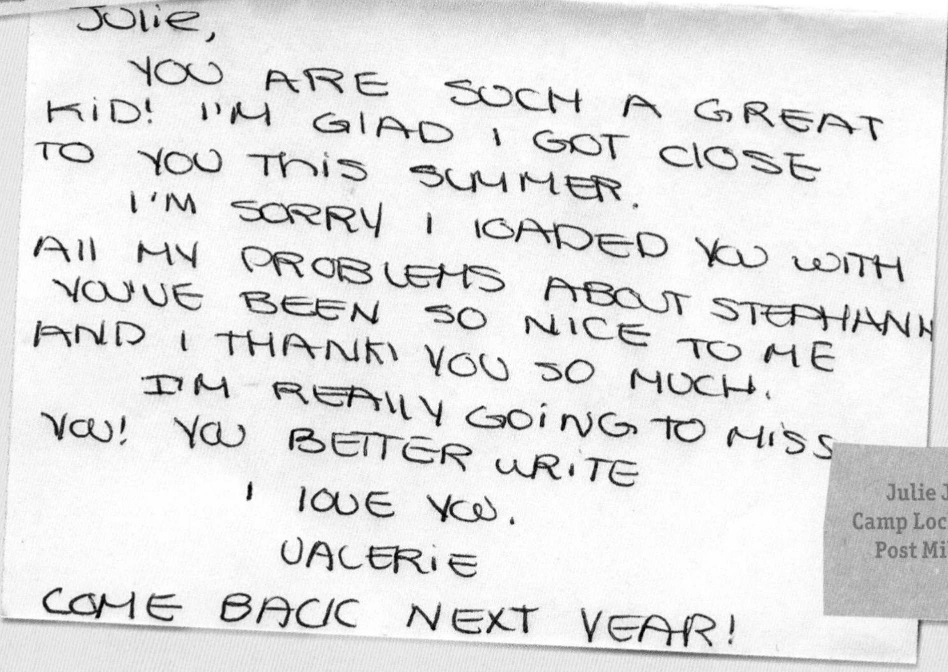

Julie,
YOU ARE SUCH A GREAT
KID! I'M GLAD I GOT CLOSE
TO YOU THIS SUMMER.
I'M SORRY I LOADED YOU WITH
ALL MY PROBLEMS ABOUT STEPHANN
YOU'VE BEEN SO NICE TO ME
AND I THANK YOU SO MUCH.
I'M REALLY GOING TO MISS
YOU! YOU BETTER WRITE
I LOVE YOU.
VALERIE
COME BACK NEXT YEAR!

Julie Jacobs
Camp Lochearn
Post Mills, VT
1982

On the last night we had a massive themed social—the last great dance of the summer. Ours was *Batman*-themed because the Tim Burton blockbuster had just been released. We spent the day making the Batmobile out of cardboard boxes, and then the nighttime feeling up girls' breasts while assuring them "I am going to miss you." For me, camp was my one opportunity to experience what it was like to be popular and athletic for six weeks each year. I'd blink and the summer would be over and it was back to reality. Back to school—sitting at the geek table in the cafeteria and getting picked last in gym class.

Adam Goldberg, Camp Echo Lark, Poyntelle, PA

Coming home was the worst depression. I would lie in bed for three weeks. This was a world without IM. No cell phone, no e-mail. I felt so powerless. The world felt so big. I would lie there flicking through the rainbows that filled my yearbook.

Jenny Weiner, Camp Emerson, Hinsdale, MA
1979

My camp years were ones of national and personal unrest. This was the time of Vietnam and Nixon. It was also when my parents got divorced. They told me they were separating right before camp. I think that is when I truly began to appreciate camp and the friendships. It was a true oasis. We would lie on our backs on a ball field at night and look up at the stars and realize how lucky we were to be there—that this place, our camp, was the greatest place on earth. Leaving camp was always devastating. For a day and a half, you would be excited to have air-conditioning. But that would quickly fade and depression would set in. We always scheduled a camp reunion within a week.

Doug Herzog, Camp Scatico, Elizaville, NY

Color War was followed by Lazy Day. After five days of staying up late writing songs and cheers and leaving it all out on the field, we got to lie in bed and do nothing, which was great practice for the rest of our lives. This was followed by Packing Day, which was another form of Lazy Day—the only real exertion needed was to write our names and nicknames on the bunk: Andrew BULL Cohen.

Andrew Goldberg, Camp Wildwood, Bridgton, ME

You would sign your name on your bunk with your boyfriend's surname as if you were married: Rachel Elizabeth Shenkman.

Rachel Sklar, Camp Winnebagoe, Muskoka, ON, Canada

The bus is about to leave. My brother looks overjoyed to be going home, while his best friend is crying.

Lauren Senderoff, Camp Echo Lark, Poyntelle, PA
1989

This was on the last day of camp. Most parents picked up their sons between 8 a.m. and 10 a.m. I had mine come around 5 p.m. That way I was able to get the full attention of all the counselors. By the time my folks came to retrieve me, I had already had heart-to-heart good-byes with most of the counselors, the kitchen staff, and two-thirds of the maintenance guys. This was setting up a lifelong need for attention at a very unhealthy level.

Perry Silver, Falling Creek Camp, Tuxedo, NC
1991

Kevin Harrison
Camp Sequoia,
Rock Hill, NY
1981

Scott Jacoby
Camp Greylock, Becket, MA
1985

Epilogue: On Behalf of All of You Who Did Not Go to Camp

FORGET IT

BY PAUL FEIG

Look, I'm the first to admit I was a neurotic kid.

I was pretty much afraid of everything.

I was a mama's boy.

I was way less mature than my peers.

I was not athletic. And I was an only child, which meant I was kinda spoiled.

So, by its very nature, camp was a virtual laundry list of things I hated most in this world:

Having to be in the sun
Having to be in the cold
Having to be in the woods
Having to wear mosquito repellant
Having to worry about snakes and bees
Having to worry about snake bites and bee stings
Having to eat at the same table with a bunch of other kids
Having to sleep in the same room with a bunch of other kids
Having to swim in cold lakes
Having to take cold showers
Having to take those showers next to other kids
Having to stand in bare feet on cold concrete while showering next to other kids

Having to get out of bed early

Having to go to bed early

Having to not watch TV

Having to sit around a campfire in the cold

Having to sing campfire songs in front of
other kids

Having to run and play sports

Having to wear shorts in public

Having to wear a swimsuit in public

Having to be away from my cat

Having to be away from my bedroom

Having to be away from my parents

Having to be away from my friends

And, worst of all, having to pretend I was
having a good time

Paul Feig
Interlochen, MI
1980

Camp to me was just one more place where the odds were good I was going to get beaten up. I got beat up in school all the time, and that was a place
where at least there were teachers and principals and hall monitors and lunch
ladies, as well as the occasional police officer to lecture us about bike safety
or tell us not to use drugs. Camp to me just seemed like some sort of lawless
Hobbesian nightmare made up of kids who became unhinged at the thought
of being unsupervised by their parents for the first time in their lives. I'd heard
all the stories about the people who were in charge of camps and they always
seemed to be about how the camp counselors were more interested in making
out with the female counselors and smoking pot than in making sure I wasn't
getting held underwater by some bullies who had decided to turn the camp into
their own personal *Lord of the Flies* theme park. I knew the cruelty of the kids
who used to beat me up at recess in the moments when the playground ladies
weren't paying attention, so I could only imagine the ass-kickings that awaited
me at some lawless Camp Survival-of-the-Fittest.

But as terrifying as the prospect of constant torment at the unwashed
hands of my peers was, the biggest horror of all was the concept of having to
use an outhouse.

Once, when I was a kid, I was taken to a friend's cabin in upper Michigan
for the weekend and learned upon arrival that there was no indoor plumbing.
When I asked my friend's mother where we were supposed to go to the bathroom, she pointed out the window to what I thought was the world's scariest

tool shed and said, "Oh, we've got a commode right there." Having never seen an outhouse before, I figured that despite its outwardly hellish appearance, once one opened the door one would find clean white tile, a sink, hand towels, potpourri, and a normal toilet. However, once I walked over and peered inside, I was horrified to find that the interior looked more like a place where a psychotic might kill and dismember streetwalkers than the usual refuge for quiet reflection and bowel evacuation that I had been brought up to believe a bathroom is supposed to be.

And so I proceeded to not go to the bathroom for two and a half days.

Sadly, the weekend I was spending with my friend's family was an extended three-day event, and after being forced to eat the massive amounts of food I was served by my friend's father, who constantly informed me that "you might be able to waste food at your house but up here the only way to leave the table is with a clean plate in front of you," I realized my digestive tract was on an unavoidable collision course with a rickety structure built over a deep dirt hole that had other people's fecal matter at the bottom.

I entered the dark and musty phone booth and was immediately hit with the stench of bowel movements past. I peered down through the hole cut into the splinter-filled plank that served as the world's most dangerous toilet seat. The small shafts of sunlight that squeezed through the gaps in the outhouse's walls dimly dappled the bottom of the five-foot-deep hole with enough illumination to make me realize I was peering into the depths of Hell. I saw what appeared to be a large collection of dark cigar-shaped objects resting at the bottom and so had to conclude that my friend's family was unfettered by any sort of gastrointestinal blockages.

If they can do it, so can you, I told myself. Just get it over with.

I took down my pants and was immediately struck with the terror that once I positioned myself over the void, something lurking in the depths might possibly reach up and yank me down through the hole by my buttocks. And so I tried to levitate over the hole like an Olympic gymnast doing a routine on the rings and tried to think about anything other than the task I was trying to perform.

It was at this delicate moment that my friend's mother suddenly pounded on the side of the outhouse like a SWAT team and yelled, "Make sure you drop a cupful of lye down the hole after you're done," literally scaring the shit out of me. "Uh . . . okay," I said in the same voice one might use if caught masturbating. "It's that white powder in the coffee can next to you," she said, realizing from my tone that I had no idea what she was talking about. "It'll help eat up what you just put down there."

The thought of having what just came out of me "eaten up" by lye made me feel a bit queasy, since in my lifetime of normal toilet encounters I had always bid farewell to my handiwork by watching it lazily spin around the clean white bowl and then travel off into the unknown, like a departing soul heading away to a "better place." But now the thought of an intimate byproduct of my own body sitting in a disease-ridden lightless pit being unceremoniously blasted with a cupful of alkaline, leaving it to dissolve horrifically like Dracula getting belted by sunlight, made me almost want to drop down into the pit and retrieve the two-and-a-half-days' worth of low-grade meals that had passed through my intestines like a cop going back for his fallen comrade. However, more motivated to escape from the reeking sweatbox that was the "commode" than to salvage one of my turds, I cleaned up as best I could with the humidity-soaked toilet tissue that hung from the wall on an ancient twisted coat hanger, tossed in a cup of lye, and got the hell out of there.

And so, the thought of reliving this nightmare at a camp surrounded by kids who could very well decide to shove me down said shithole like the kid hiding from the Nazis in *Schindler's List* was more than I could even consider.

And so I never went to camp.

Did I miss out? I don't know. But I have to say that, even to this day, if the movie *Meatballs* comes on the TV, I always watch it with a small twinge of sadness. Because it always makes camp look like it might have been a sort of fun place to go for a week or two.

CONTRIBUTORS

One of the singular pleasures of this project has been hearing the tall tales that recapture the details of the camp experience. We are indebted to the following, who rose to the task with the gusto last exhibited by Michelangelo once he was offered the chance to paint the Sistine Chapel. We are grateful to each and every one of you.

Stuart Blumberg is a writer and producer of films including *Keeping the Faith* and *The Girl Next Door*. He lives in New York and is still trying to recapture those halcyon summer days at Camp Modin when time seemed to slow to a halt.

Jamie Denbo is a native Bostonian, actress, comedian, and writer currently working and living in Los Angeles with her husband, John. She misses singing loudly with a large group of girls during flagpole at Camp Tel Noar in New Hampshire. Sometimes she sees a flag and just starts singing loudly until her husband punches her arm.

Paul Feig retired from the world of camping and went on to a career as an actor, writer, and director, in addition to creating the TV show *Freaks and Geeks*. He currently directs both television and feature films, and has written two memoirs, *Kick Me* and *Superstud,* along with the young adult book *Ignatiaus McFarland: Frequenaut.*

Adam Goldberg is a TV and film writer whose credits include *The Muppet Wizard of Oz, Fanboys,* and *The Jetsons*. What he misses most about camp: scoring a Chunky bar at canteen, midnight raids to the girls' side, and making a box-stitch gimp bracelet for his special lady friend. What he misses least about camp: his foot accidentally touching the bottom of the lake.

Andrew Goldberg is a writer for *Family Guy*. The part of camp he misses most is being allowed to go commando in a pair of lacrosse shorts without it becoming an "HR issue."

Alex Grossman is a writer living in Los Angeles. His fondest memories of camp include his first kiss, both real and imagined.

AJ Jacobs is the author of *The Know-It-All: One Man's Humble Quest to Become the Smartest Person in the World* and *The Year of Living Biblically: One Man's Humble Quest to Follow the Bible as Literally as Possible.* He misses the fluorescent green tubes of Prell shampoo.

Nick Kroll has starred in network sitcoms, co-created an amazing book, contributed pop culture nonsense for TV and public radio, and written and performed for critically acclaimed sketch shows, but his greatest accomplishment was when he mooned all the girls of Camp Tapawingo after a particularly uneventful social.

David Lubliner is a senior vice president in the motion picture literary department at the William Morris Agency. He lives in Los Angeles with his wife, Stacey, and his two-year-old son, Andrew, whom he plans to send to camp someday very soon. He misses the occasional pizza parties we had late at night in our bunks when a counselor would bring back food from the local pizzeria, called the Bristol House Of Pizza (aka the BHOP). It was only a pizza, but it was like eating the finest food in the world when all we knew was shepherd's pie and fruit punch all summer long.

Ross Martin is senior vice president and head of programming for mtvU, MTV's twenty-four-hour Emmy Award winning college network, reaching over 7 million college students nationwide. He is also author of the book, *The Cop Who Rides Alone*. He misses bug juice, bunk-hopping and believing he was once a badass for at least a summer.

Molly Rosen is a writer who lives in the East Village. She misses singing "The Dock of the Bay" naked in her sleeping bag on Cinnamon Bun Sunday mornings.

Todd Rosenberg (aka Odd Todd) is an animator and writer who runs the website oddtodd.com. He is the author of *The Odd Todd Handbook: Hard Times, Soft Couch* and frequently provides "humorous" animation for ABC's *World News Tonight*. He is currently working on stuff. The thing he misses about camp (besides the archery) is the smells.

Rodney Rothman is the author of the bestselling memoir *Early Bird*. He has also published work in *The New York Times, The New Yorker, GQ, McSweeney's* and the *New York Times Magazine*. While he was head writer of *The Late Show with David Letterman,* the show won two Emmy awards for Best Show. *Forgetting Sarah Marshall,* a film he is writing for and producing, will be released by Universal Pictures in the spring of 2009. What he misses most from camp are all-white, all-Jewish productions of *The Wiz*.

Rebecca Shapiro is the director of publicity at Shore Fire Media, a public relations firm with expertise in music, entertainment, and popular culture. She and her husband, Peter, a music and film producer, reside in Manhattan with their daughter, Roxy. Rebecca misses the powdered vanilla pudding she so enjoyed during her camping adventures near the waters of Camp Manito-wish in Northern Wisconsin. However, she does not miss picking the bugs out of her pudding or portaging her canoe.

Rachel Sklar is a writer, blogger, and editor in New York and the author of *Jew-ish: Who We Are, How We Got Here, and All the Ish In Between* (HarperCollins, 2008). She misses many things about camp, but most of all she misses how totally acceptable it was to do her job in a bikini. Now, for some reason, they frown upon that.

Evan Turner is a vice president of production and development at Walden Media in Los Angeles. What he misses most about camp: neon Umbros, under-the-shirt over-the-bra action, and slow dancing to the Phil Collins classic "Don't Let Him Steal Your Heart Away." What he misses least about camp: coming home.

David Wain is a director, writer, comedian and actor, best known for the TV shows *Stella* and *The State* and the movies *The Ten* and the summer camp comedy *Wet Hot American Summer*. What he misses most about camp: getting sweaty at sunset, playing Frisbee, or doing whatever.

WHERE ARE THEY NOW?

We have sought to credit everyone involved in this project. If we've erred or omitted anyone, please let us know so we can make the necessary changes to future editions.

William "Wil-Dog" Abers is a bassist for Ozomatli and is based in Los Angeles. **Matthew Adler** lives in Miami Beach, FL, and is a real estate developer. **Kevin Asch** is a film director and producer who lives in Santa Monica, CA. **Hillary Goldrich Auster** lives in New York with her husband and is getting her Master's in public health and nutrition. **Sara Barron** is a writer and comedian in New York and the author of *People Are Unappealing: True Stories of Our Collective Capacity to Irritate and Annoy* (Random House). **Stacy Bass** is a magazine and fine art photographer who lives in Connecticut. Her son just finished his first summer at Birchmont, where he is third-generation. **Deb Bander** lives in Miami and practices law. **Barbi Stalburg Bell** lives in Birmingham, Michigan. She and her husband, Kenny, have two kids, ages 3 and 4. **Jamie Ben** is a stay-at-home mom who lives in West Bloomfield, MI. **Nigel Bennett** runs a real estate consultancy in Liverpool, England. **Vanessa Kroll Bennett** lives in New York City with her two beautiful sons and the world's most nostalgic man. **Amy Blackman** lives in Los Angeles and manages her favorite bands as part of Tsunami Entertainment, is married to a Nicaraguan chef, and berates herself daily for not being fluent in Spanish. **Josh Bernstein** travels and explores the world, hosting a series and executive-producing for the Discovery Channel. **Aaron Bisman** established JDub, a not-for-profit label and event production company for new Jewish culture. **Jason F. Boschan** is a real estate agent for both residential and commercial property in Charlotte, NC. **Alan Bowes** still dreams of one day returning to camp and winning the Boys Under-14 Softball Championship. He currently resides in New York City. **Mark Boxer** lives in Armonk, NY, and is the vice president of sales for the Independent Film Channel. **Ariel Brooke Silberman** lives in New York City with her husband, Lewis. She is an actress and producer. **Hal Brooks** is a theater director who lives in Boerum Hill, Brooklyn. **Sharon Brous** is the rabbi at a new spiritual community—IKAR—in Los Angeles. **Evan Cohen** is a film producer and entertainment marketing executive who lives and works in Los Angeles. **Jon Cohen** is the cofounder of *The Fader* magazine and Cornerstone. He lives and works in New York City with his wife Caryn and two kids. **Michael Cohen** is a Gooner who lives in Brooklyn and runs Deaf Dumb & Blind Communications, a multifaceted entertainment and lifestyle company. **Rachel Leah Cohen** is an actress in Los Angeles. **Jim Cone** lives in Los Angeles and no longer gets homesick. **Sloane Crosley** lives in New York and works in book publishing. She is the author of *I Was Told There'd Be Cake* (Riverhead Books) and also wrote the cover story for the worst-selling issue of *Maxim* in the magazine's history. **Melissa Brown Eisenberg** lives in New York and is a new mom to a daughter, Elliot, and wife to Jason. **Adam Epstein** lives in New York and works in theater. **Jenna Fallon** works for Nike and lives in Portland, OR, with her husband, Eric. She is still best of friends with camper Hillary Goldrich-Auster. **Josh Frank** is a writer of books and screenplays who lives in Austin, TX. **Ken Freimann** is an agent living in Los Angeles. **Deborah Gitell**, proud aunt of Max Gitell and a Big Police Fan, lives in West Hollywood and works for alloy media + marketing. **Doug Grad** is a senior editor at a major New York publishing house who lives in Brooklyn with his wife, Kim, and children, Amanda and Harry. **Brad Grossman** is an executive at Imagine Entertainment in Los Angeles. **Kevin "Bird" Harrison** is an inventory planner/account executive for a sunglasses manufacturer. He currently resides in West Orange, NJ, with his beautiful wife, Ilisa, and his darling daughter, Ella. **Lori Harrison** is an attorney who lives in New York City. She still sees her camp friends on a weekly basis and considers them among her closest friends. **Todd Hasak-Lowy** is a professor and writer who lives in Gainesville, FL. **Julie Hermelin** is a writer/director who lives with her husband, Mitchell, and three sons in Los Angeles. She is no longer quite as new wave, although some people who know her might disagree. **David Hertog** is not a member of the NRA. He's a marketing director for an Internet company in New York City. **Doug Herzog** lives in Los Angeles, is president of the entertainment group at MTV Networks and still occasionally dreams that he is going to camp. **Stacy Horne** is an event producer who lives in Brooklyn and San Francisco. **Courtney William Holt** leads digital for MTV Networks Music Group and lives in New York City with his wife and two kids, Stella and Sammy. **Amy Israel** is the executive vice president of production and acquisitions at Paramount Vantage. She lives in Los Angeles with her husband, RD Robb, and her daughter, Zoë. **Andrew Jacobs** is a reporter at the *New York Times* and a documentary film director who lives in New York City. **Julie Schoenberg Jacobs** lives in New York City with her husband and three sons. She is the director of sales and marketing for Watson Adventures Scavenger Hunts, which puts her camp counselor skills to good use. **Scott Jacoby** is a Grammy Award–winning music producer, engineer, songwriter, recording artist and is the CEO and founder of Eusonia Records. **Mitch Kamin** is the president and CEO of Bet Tzedek Legal Services, a nonprofit law firm that serves low-income seniors, families, and Holocaust survivors. **David Katznelson** is a Record Man and provincial equestrian who resides in

San Francisco (Go Giants!). **David Kohan** is a television writer who lives in Los Angeles. **Lily Koppel** is a writer who lives in New York City. **Dana Kroll** lives in New York City and wishes she could wear camp uniform to work everyday. **Ilana Edelman Kunstanowitz** is a school psychologist who lives in Manhattan. **Simmy Kustanowitz** uses his camp counselor skills every day as a writer at MTV. **Jordan Kurland** is a longtime resident of San Francisco, CA. He is the owner of Zeitgeist Artist Management and co-owner of Noise Pop Festival. **Mark Lamster** graduated from Camp Tomahawk's Commanche Commando Attack Force (CCAF) and is currently at work on a history of the political career of Peter Paul Rubens. **Gillian Laub** is a photographer in New York City. **Karen Lauterstein** has a career in sales and lives in downtown New York City. She still keeps in close contact with her camp friends (especially L.G. and Sammy B.) and will always be a camper at heart. **Kate Lee** is a literary agent who lives in New York City. **Heidi Lender** is a writer, editor, and yoga teacher living in San Francisco. **Dany Levy** lives in New York City and is the founder, chairman and editor-in-chief of DailyCandy, Inc. **Georgia Liebman** is an art director who lives in Boston. **David Light** is a comedy writer, married to a camp girl. They live in Los Angeles. **Brenda Wolkstein Lowenberg** is a math teacher and tutor who lives in Audubon, PA. **Shana Madoff** is an attorney who lives in Manhattan. She is married and has a daughter named Rebecca. **Stacy Marcus** is a designer who lives in New York City. **David Measer** lives in Los Angeles and works at an ad agency and refuses to sleep outside. **Eric Michaels** is an attorney living in Bloomfield Hills, MI, with his wife, Jenny, and two beautiful children, Kate and Ryan. **Mark Miller** is a financial planning specialist with Smith Barney in New York City. He lives with his wife, Kim, in Scarsdale, NY, and their five-year-old pug named Virgil. **Mik Moore** is the director of communications and public policy at Jewish Funds for Justice and lives in New York City with his wife, Deborah, and two children. **Eddy Portnoy** is the operator of a large chutney locker in Williamsburg, Brooklyn, and lives in New York, whatever. **Eileen Quast** is a triplet mom and directs public relations for TNT, TBS, and TCM. **Erika Reff Vogel** lives in New York City with her husband, Jon. The lanyard-bracelet-making skills she learned at camp have paid off. She is now the director of the Association of Israel's Decorative Arts. **Gabbi Robinson Promoff** is a mother-to-be and a public health analyst who lives in Atlanta, GA, and works at the Centers for Disease Control and Prevention. **Mark Ronson** makes songs and lives in Greenwich Village. **Matthew Rosen** is a broker who lives in New York City. **Laser Rosenberg** lives in Los Angeles and is a multi media artist and designer working on a book of his own collage artworks. www.laserrosenberg.com. **Tom Rosenberg** is an attorney-at-law who lives in Columbus, OH. **Brice Rosenbloom** is a music producer in Brooklyn. **Katie Rosman** is a journalist who lives in Manhattan. **Douglas Ross** is a producer of nonfiction television shows who lives in Los Angeles, California. **Jordan Roter** wrote *Camp Rules* (Dutton) and lives in Los Angeles. **Lauren Sandler** is a journalist and editor living in Brooklyn, and the author of *Righteous: Dispatches from the Evangelical Youth Movement*. **David Sax** is a journalist and writer who lives in Toronto while working on a book about the death of the Jewish delicatessen. **Katie Weinberg Schumacher** lives with her husband, Patrick, and daughter, Ashley, in Short Hills, NJ. **Ellen Schweber** lives in Old Westbury, NY, and works as an art consultant. **Emily Selden** works in higher education in Chicago, IL, and wishes she weren't too old to still spend summers at camp. **Lauren Senderoff** is a mom who can not wait to send her daughter to sleepaway camp and lives in Bloomington, IN. **Sari Sharaby** is a senior financial analyst at the Guggenheim Museum who just got married, but not to someone from camp. **Debbie Shell** works in sales for America Online Media Network and is also the founder of The Tutor Tree, a supplemented-education company in California. **Perry Silver** is an actor who lives in Manhattan. **Sarah Rubin Sokolic** is a New York-based actor and educator and is the associate executive director of Storahtelling, Inc., a Jewish ritual theater company. **Sara Solfanelli** is a lawyer who lives in Manhattan. **Michael Solomon**, an editor at ESPN Books, still doesn't believe the 1982 Color War at Camp Androscoggin ended in a tie. **Matt Spitz** is a bookstore manager who lives in Durham, NC. **Lauren Stein** is a television executive who lives in Los Angeles. **Jon Steingart** lives in New York City, is a theater and film producer, and cofounded Jewcy. **Liz Stevens**, a former journalist, recently joined her parents, Larry and Ina Stevens, as an assistant director at Camp Walden in Michigan. **Jason Strauss** is cofounder of the Strategic Group, a multifaceted marketing, special events, and promotion company that runs New York's venerable Marquee and the nightclub at Tao Las Vegas. **Andrew Strickman** is a marketing executive and freelance journalist and lives in San Francisco and also teaches at 826 Valencia, a writing center for children. **Jake Sussman** is a criminal defense attorney who lives in Charlotte, N.C. **Lisa Wainer** is the director of special events for the YMCA of Greater New York. She lives in New York City. **Adam Wallach** is an account executive at a media buying company who is happily married (to a Camp Ramah alum) and lives in Manhattan. **Lindsay Weiss** is an event producer living in New York City. **Jenny Wiener** is a producer who lives in New York City with her husband, Jon Steingart, and their children, Leo and Ruby. **Rick Wisniewski,** aka "Wiz," is a technology consultant for Westlaw who lives in Dallas, TX, with his wife, three kids, and three dogs. **Julia Wolov** is a comedian who lives in Los Angeles. **Claire Zulkey** is a writer who lives in Chicago. You can learn more about her at the website Zulkey.com.

ACKNOWLEDGMENTS

As ever, we are deeply indebted to the thousands of people who took the time to share their photographs and stories with us. As far as we are concerned, they should all be in the Smithsonian. We are particularly grateful to all those who were willing to sit down face-to-face and dredge up every minute detail of camp life remaining in the memory banks. It was a privilege to listen. We are in awe of all of those who rose to the challenge and contributed essays—stories of heroism and courage against the odds. You are all our heroes and we are honored and grateful. Two people went above and beyond: Paul Feig, for vibing with this project even though he hated camp, and Adam Goldberg, who would win a gold medal if the Olympics had a competition for the best ratio of hilarious stories to stories told. Finally, having Ivan Reitman write such a personal foreword was our equivalent of working with whomever wrote the Bible. *Meatballs* will forever be one of the definitive movies in our world, and is canonical when it comes to summer camp. We are indebted to Mr. Reitman, as well as to Andrea Hirschegger and Violet and Harold Ramis for helping make our dream come true.

Thanks again to the mothers of America. We love each and every one of you—especially those who were sent into the attic on bold solo missions to unearth albums left behind by offspring who have long since fled the nest. In particular, we have to thank Sonya Miller, mother of Mark, for having a sense of humor and letting us use the letters on pages 126 and 127, which are belied by the fact that she is an amazing mother who did write to her son a lot, and Susan Fallon, Jenna's mom, writer of one of the most beautiful letters we have ever seen.

Thanks to all who have helped pull this project off from the inside. This has been an exhausting process and would not have been possible without the passionate support of Michelle Jaslow and her Web diligence, Zsolt Sarvary-Bene for his photographic work, Brian Huizingh for technical support, *Entertainment Weekly* for picking the project up so quickly and helping the contributions flow in, and Ned Rosenthal and Cabot Marks for legal advice. Dana Ferine, you are one of the most amazing people we have ever worked with. Your tireless patience, attention to detail, and great sense of humor have been *Guinness World Records*—worthy throughout. Kippi Rai Spraggon, you are also a killer and are deeply missed. Our designers, Marco and Anne Cibola at Novestudio, are magnificent giants, two of the most creative, process-driven, and calm individuals we could partner with. Everyone in the world should work with you on all projects—and can do via www.novestudio.com.

Working with our editor, Carrie Thornton, with the assistance of Brandi Bowles, Erin LaCour, Min Lee, and everyone at Crown, has been a massive pleasure. Thanks for all of your encouragement, patience, care, and spot-on feedback. Kate Lee, superagent at ICM, thanks for your guidance. Your support is total and you consistently give the smartest advice a client could want to hear.

Roger Bennett would like to thank:

From a camping perspective, thanks to all of the following for their strategic and creative advice, patience, and support: Alex and Caren Kurtz Goodman, AJ and Julie Jacobs, Jon and Caryn Cohen and all at Cornerstone, Jason Strauss, Ross Martin, Rachel Sklar, Mark Ronson, Doug Herzog, Gillian Laub, Karen Lauterstein, Michael Cohen at Deaf Dumb & Blind, Naomi Less at the amazing Foundation for Jewish Camping, Stephen Clare at Campgroup LLC, the gents at Bunk1.com, Sarah Herman at Windsor Mountain, and JC Smith at Henry Jacobs. Also thanks to the following for creating three amazing pieces of camp culture that inspired us. They deserve to be Amazon-ed by one and all: Josh Wolk's *Cabin Pressure* (Hyperion), Jordan Roter's *Camp Rules* (Dutton), and David Wain's masterpiece, *Wet Hot American Summer*.

Thanks to the following for all of their support throughout the writing process: Juan Valdez, Everton FC, the wait staff at Gino's (60th and Lexington), all at ACBP, especially CRB, the late great AMB, and Jeffrey Solomon, as well as Rachel Levin. Courtney Holt, Josh Kun, David Katznelson (and all at Birdman Records) at Reboot Stereophonic, David Hirshey and Michael Solomon and everyone at ESPN Books, Eli Horowitz and Ping-Pong players around the world, Howard Jacobson, Roland Scahill, David Lubliner, and Ken Freimann at William Morris, Adam Epstein, Andrew Miano, the *Guilt & Pleasure* magazine team, the inventors of foosball and seltzer (I am assuming they are two different people), Hippo and Campus at www.hippocampusmusic.com, and everyone working on *And You Shall Know Us by the Trail of Our Vinyl,* David Moyes, Dan Harverd, Jonni Bertfield, my lovely Mum and Dad, Nigel, Amy, Holly (R.I.P.), Simmy and the Kirsches, all of the Kroll Family, Celia Dollar, and Jamie Glassman (will the *Zulu* rewrite ever be finished?) from the sandbox to the grave.

I am fortunate to be a member of the Academy of the Recent Past (www.acadamyoftherecentpast. com), an organization whose camaraderie is magnificent, and to have attended Camp Kingswood in Bridgton, Maine, which was one of the most formative experiences in my life. Deb Gitell, you rock. Jeff Barron, if you read this, please be in touch. Above all, infinite love and gratitude to Samson, Ber, and my wife, Vanessa, for believing in me and being the equivalent of a Color War General every day of my life.

Phil Collins, I may have used one of your songs as a chapter title but I still want to fight you.

Jules Shell would like to thank:

All of you who willingly entrusted us with your golden camp memories (you know who you are). My camp boyfriend of five summers, Brad, who aspired to be in politics when he grew up, so I spared him the grief of appearing in this book. And with great thanks to Vic and Craig at Camp Tamakwa and to Liz, Scott, Larry, Ina, Buffy, and Eric from Camp Walden. May the memory of Neal Schechter leading the Three Wooden Pigeons cheer in the mess hall live on forever.

Boggy,
...s the best
...er, and I'm
...ppy I spent
my best
...d in the
...d. H was
...edible. H
...amazing.

...ace
Out!

Dear Boggy,
It was a great summer.
You had JR.
I had JR.
JL had TS.
ME had X.
TM had X.

You are a great friend and a great guy. You are one of my best friends in camp. I look forward to the random phone conversations. I'm sure there will be many laughter with you there are always many laughs and good times.

Peace Out,

I'm here at 60MTHEWER U BOGGY- This summer ...
... of fun. I'm upset that it's ...
R that this year you're going to ...
So you'll get my letters. ...
first guitar teacher. So, I ...
of you. I'm always be the b...
...amph, even if U don't Sh...
was a blast. So was enter...
Thanks for always being...
best friends and favoring...
of my 7 years here...
keep in touch...
I'm st...

Snoop BO

Tha...
one ...
Hangin...
best ...
We ...
You ...
for ...

Dear Boggy,
I had a great summer w/you.
I felt like I sort of belonged w/you this year.
Hopefully, we'll stay in touch this winter. I'm so happy you got into USA. Everything worked out perfectly

P.S. Next summer in Newport

Sleepy

Love,

great. Your hared ...
where o learn os ...
the camp d kids cam...

Boggy)
The 500 is good
but Mansfield is the best
Thanx for giving me a great senior year.
Rob S. Bush

Dear Boggy/

Thanx for making
my summer better.
The times we chilled
together were...
I look forward
keeping in touch
over the winter
And don't forget
to come back to
have sex with

Boggy-
Your the
Best! Sorry
HH you for w...
me up! Call N...
From Georgi...
Have a good
Winter.
Easy.

being
best friends.

...you was the
the summer.
...ep in touch.
visit. Thanks
my summer
...e ya in Georgia.
the Wiese.
ROSS

Stay Real,
Dave
Sherman

I'm glad that we've finally
friends after all these years.
Hopefully, we'll keep in touch
the winter. Georgia is lucky to
have you there. Have a great
Lihick

By Roger Bennett,
Jules Shell, and Nick Kroll

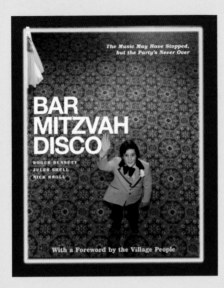

978-1-4000-8044-1
$23.95 (Canada: $33.95)
Available wherever
books are sold.

Crown Publishers
New York
www.crownpublishing.com

Add to the Academy's Archives

The Academy of the Recent Past is dedicated to rummaging through the flotsam and jetsam of our lives. We are inspired by tales of the ordinary. Bar Mitzvahs and summer camp are just the tip of the iceberg. Find out how to contribute to the Academy and be a part of our projects.

ACADEMY
OF THE
RECENT PAST

www.academyoftherecentpast.com